A Few Poets on Rod Jellema

On *The Lost Faces*

His steadiness of vision — a sense of forward searching in his developing body of work — shows up, I think, in *The Lost Faces*. . . . Experience is adding to the depth and seriousness of the poems, and this without diluting an alertness, a zest and gusto, apparent earlier on.

— William Stafford

A superb piece of work. . . . A set of poems entirely remarkable for the physical pungency of their language, their muscular and sensitive rhythms, their power of creating a particular world in its real time and place. Some of the poems are positively harrowing in their effectiveness, the truth and depth of their feeling, which, of course, can only be revealed by the most careful, intelligent craftsmanship.

— James Wright

What is new and comparatively rare in poets is his discovery that a lyrical impulse and a meditative urgency may alternate, feed off each other, disguise themselves as each other. . . . Supple technique accommodates process. . . . [The poems] show a technique forged from confrontation with the demands of content to become formal. That is what good poets can do and less good poets can never arrange.

— William Matthews

On *A Slender Grace*

Rod Jellema, like most mystics, starts small and ends large. He looks into a dryer in a Laundromat and suddenly he is at the river, pounding on his clothes with a rock — past and present merged. He looks at a green bean and sees "the holy scent of turned earth/slendered into a bean." But he is a mystic who never becomes mystical; he never loses touch with the earth. He is a poet of deep and humane good sense who's infused with an abiding awareness of the holy. There is much more than a slender grace in *A Slender Grace.*

— Andrew Hudgins

Rod Jellema regards a various world with love and patience, and records with energetic precision his encounters with it. His sense of a brief instant's emotional weight is unerring.

— Henry Taylor

Today, with our human species on the brink of various political-ecological catastrophes, we look for poetry that faces the worst and earns its own being. Rod Jellema's *Slender Grace* spares us nothing of our searing knowledge of Treblinka, or of the ravaged villagers of Nicaragua, or of the persecution of artistic spirit, or of our mania in the Middle East. His intuitive need in this "age of glare" for redemptive mystery and darkness, as this need generates his poems, is profound and moving. This is a strong, welcome, consoling book.

— William Heyen

INCARNALITY
The Collected Poems

Rod Jellema

WILLIAM B. EERDMANS PUBLISHING COMPANY

GRAND RAPIDS, MICHIGAN / CAMBRIDGE, U.K.

Published 2010 by

Wm. B. Eerdmans Publishing Co.

2140 Oak Industrial Drive N.E., Grand Rapids, Michigan 49505 /

P.O. Box 163, Cambridge CB3 9PU U.K.

Printed in the United States of America

16 15 14 13 12 11 10   7 6 5 4 3 2 1

Library of Congress Cataloging-in-Publication Data

Jellema, Roderick.

    Incarnality: the collected poems / Rod Jellema.

          p.   cm.

    ISBN 978-0-8028-2749-4 (pbk.: alk. paper)

    I. Title.

    PS3560.E465I53   2010

    811'.54 — dc22

                       2010033377

www.eerdmans.com

to

Michele: boundless thanks.

and for

David and Michael: a father's blessing.

Contents

From *The Eighth Day: Poems New and Selected* (1984)

Interlude: Translations

From *A Slender Grace* (2004)

Still . . .   Later Poems, 2005-2010

Preface: A Book of Poems in Search of a Title

The present custom is to publish poetry collections as "Selected and New" or "New and Selected" poems. This book does indeed select older poems and contain new ones. It is called "Collected Poems" because I have gathered into it from earlier books only those poems that I now know were on their way to forming this one unified book. Its forty-nine new poems, a kind of rounding off but in no way a "conclusion," helped me to explore and see and then extend the book's wholeness.

The many poems from my earlier books that I have kept out of this collection were often stepping stones toward it but finally not part of it. I like that my "collected" is unusually slender.

What kept needling me while making poems after forty was a growing insistence from somewhere within them that these poems must refuse to rocket-thrust the experience of soul and spirit heavenward into the mists and gasses, beyond sight, into pure unstained light, away from the good heft of the physical.

Making poems is my way of clarifying and seeing. As a teacher I needed that. I have been watching how our culture has trivialized the mysterious image of light, so much so that its ubiquitous glare blinds us to our need for some positive darkness. In the same way, I mistrust the tendency, gaining favor presently in our culture, to regard physical objects, things, bodies as inferior stuff that we must transcend. To struggle as we aspire toward spiritual enlightenment is to put aside the other possibility: that the spiritual takes the initiative, comes down to us, dwells in our time and history and flesh. In many mythologies as well as in Christian belief, the eternal Divine descends, assumes human form, and thereby sanctifies time and the physical. This is a clear choice: whether to appropriate and enjoy and conserve the world or to flee it.

More and more, my work has come to be celebratory. Good fertile darkness and lively physicality are often the subjects celebrated. If this seems unusual, I hope it is so for the unusual moments of discovery, the jolts of surprise. Darkness, after all, is not only ignorance, fear, and evil; it is the mystery in which we dream and imagine and create; it is, science tells us, 85 percent of the stuff of the universe. And the physical is not just "carnality" — wickedly alluring fleshpots or sensual distractions from white light and pure spirit; the physical is the astonishing home in which spirit lives.

I like the effect of reversing now and then the values of light and dark. I also like the effect of celebrating human bodies, graceful motion, nature, and I am fascinated by the ways in which literary writers and other artists can incarnate their perceptions and their vision into the physical stuff of print, paint, and music. So I see this book as a kind of carnival, a festival of the sort that James Thomson defined in 1744 as one in which "the glad Circle . . . yield their Souls to festive mirth."

I'd like my carnival to have the zest and color and blaring of New Orleans' Mardi Gras or the old Carnival of Venice. Let it hum its praise for the surprise of God-made-flesh that endows all humans, and mix that with its celebration of standing ribs of roast beef served with burgundy wine. Hallelujah for *carne.* Let hot carnival lights shoot in vain for stars far off into the embracing, cool darkness.

But unlike that rush of carnival days before Lent (indulgence before the ritual of abstinence), this is a lasting carnival, for all time, giving thanks for the astonishing realization that spirit, "the breath of God," is in residence here and now.

And then there is also this: the need for the soul's lamentations from a corner of the beribboned tent, noting the sad confusions and misunderstandings among us about things carnal and things incarnate.

I have to use a rare, seldom-used word for what I see and miss and celebrate: *Incarnality.* It gradually became the title of this book. The few theologians who use the term mean something profoundly philosophical; I mean it to suggest all the hungry, thirsty, leaping excitement of carnival-time, but as a year-round and forever celebration of the temporal, physical, finite, material world. That world is created as an expression of and a container for the timeless and spiritual. Just as the infinite is within us humans — reflected as idea, vision, thought, imagination — so it is embodied by the physical world, giving us glimpses of the wonder and life-force that are enfleshed in it.

That's what Incarnality is about. It's about seeking and traveling until you get to a strange place called home and discover you belong there. Necessarily, of course, it also tries to catch the feel of a world in which that way seems missing and is sometimes longed for. But I like absence, the very presence of absence. Likewise, in an age which honors bigness, I have been catching splinters, threads, narrow light rays, flashes — moments of awareness of forces that we see only partially. In an age of glitter and glare, I try to sense the healthy need for the mystery of darkness. In an age that creates, for its pleasure or distraction, the unreal heavens of sentimental pop songs and TV, and the cloying honey of sympathy cards, and the childish cartoon heavens afloat in puffy clouds, I try to see in the here-and-now pieces and fragments of a very physical Eden. It wants rebuilding.

This book is not an argument in the service of a thesis. It strings together moments of experience or awareness that took shape as poems in the process of my making them. Willa Cather's phrase is right: "Touch and pass on." I hope they are a lively reminder that making poems is simply an alternate way of seeing. Take a look and pass on.

ROD JELLEMA
Washington, D.C.
June 7, 2010

Double Vision

Most of us leave school believing that poems are intimidating and distant, addressed to the few. So poets would seem to have some special fire that sets them apart and leaves everyone else behind. It's not so. Their difference from everyone else is that, encountering things or people or experiences, they take a second look. And then their poems invite others to share that second look.

It may take poets a long time and some hard work to focus that second look and then correlate it with the first glance, the mere appearance. Like painters, they may link the second look to history or ideas, to associations or images that didn't occur to you on first look as you hastened on your way. But they see the same stuff that you see, and in the same way, 99 percent of the time. Don't be put off by the poets' one percent. They take time to catch a kind of double vision of this or that thing, this or that moment of awareness — simply because it's fascinating. They try with words to catch that fascination. Each poem that survives its own process of being made beckons you back for a few minutes to have another look. If it looks unlike what you're accustomed to — good, that's the point. You don't have to analyze it; just let it do its work. And its work is to *make* experience in some fresh and direct way rather than to exult over it or chat about it or explain it. If you force a poem into talking your kind of talk, it loses everything in the translation.

In Ireland they speak of "thin places," where only the mists divide this world from the Other. When I'm writing to catch that second look, clarifying gradually what it becomes as I try to make it, the backdrop against which I see the world around us is Eden, the lost Eden, almost invisible and always fragmented and splintered, but enough of a presence so that I can sometimes draw on it, play it into the process of what I make. I want to edge up to such slender moments when I can, and then give them heft and substance, ground them — ground them at the very least in the way we ground electricity.

(Condensed and revised version of the preface to *A Slender Grace*)

On that exciting second look, even the long-accepted symbols of our culture can change. It is not entirely strange to the wisdom of our time, for example, to reverse now and then the values of light and dark. Recalling the tens of thousands of people blinded by the flash at Hiroshima, we should recall for contrast Moses at Sinai approaching "the thick darkness . . . where God was."

This making of poems is really not such a goofy or precious or starry-eyed thing to do. Humans try to create because they're human, because they are made in the image of their Creator. We all recognize some creative longings and stirrings in ourselves: that fading Polaroid snapshot of the old Latin teacher, or the postcard you wrote from Viet Nam, don't quite do or say what you want them to. There are auras of implication you didn't explore. You see such implications sometimes in the swaying of an ice-covered branch, in a mysterious movement of words and their sounds through certain phrases, in a strange aware-ness that can move us when we remember a lost schoolmate or hear breaking waves in the distance.

For the cosmic minute or two of our history, cut out of millions of years, we're living in the eighth day of creation. The world is still being created, but now it's our job. We all create (or sometimes destroy) with our lives, but some go on creating the world in more special ways — trying to finish the job, Van Gogh would say — by imaging forth what's beneath and behind our lives.

*   *   *

The poems that I write come out of the workings of such double vi-sion. But because my second looks involve the Judeo-Christian belief in a lost Paradise, and in seeing that lost world as the impetus for rebuilding this one, it might be assumed that this book is a collec-tion of religious poems. Well, any potential reader thumbing through these pages can notice that there are many poems which seem not "religious" at all. That's as it should be. The Christian faith is the lump of yeast stirred into the dough that makes the whole loaf, the book of poems, what it is. I don't want to dish out dollops of raw yeast, and you shouldn't want to ingest them. Let's let the yeast per-meate the loaf.

So these poems individually are not spiritual message-bearers. They are poems, seeing double. It is inevitable that my belief in a beautiful world which is broken and divinely redeemed, though I am not preaching about it, should be yeasting and working throughout. It is simply my way of seeing.

The poems of mine that hold religious themes — being not at home in the present world, seeing how narrowly we almost miss God's grace, feeling awe for the dark, exploring God's incarnation in Christ as the archetypal figure for seeing ourselves and physical things as well as the arts as lesser embodiments of the spiritual — are obviously "religious." But I want to insist, in the name of human creativeness, that these thematic guidelines weigh less than the little reflections of my interest in people, words, memory, scenery, flashes of awareness — not "reported" but created in a process. The poetry is the thing that (note the word) *matters.*

The world out there, certainly on second look, shimmers with ripe implications and little metaphysical nudges. My work as a poet and teacher has tried respectfully to challenge both prosaic realism and poetic spiritualism by mingling the real and the supernatural, by making them inter-related and sometimes indivisible.

The life of the mind must, I think, draw sustenance from a mix of the ethereal and the earthy, the carnal and the eternal, moved by flashes and echoes of Eden's physicality. I mean these poems to feel the tug toward a fully spiritual world, and then to share some responsibility for the beautiful broken world that some of us, mistakenly, would flee. I want them to speak quietly of survival. I mean them to be sometimes celebratory, and always offering the reader the pleasure of seeing double.

ROD JELLEMA
Washington, D.C.
January 6, 2004
May 22, 2010

From *Something Tugging the Line* (1974)

Watch for Deer Crossing

the yellow signs say.
I do. The deer
aren't there. But once

I drove up Lakeshore Drive
in a blind blizzard of sleep
and had to brake

fast and hard
at the sign.
I watched horses,

rhinos, a dinosaur cross
my yellow path,
moving inland.

I keep watching
hoping I am reading
the right signs.

Mrs. Van Den Bosch

I was in her dark house next door just once,
and she gave me a cookie. She used to catch rain
in a shiny silver tub; it slid down so clean
I think Mr. Van Den Bosch scrubbed their roof
every week with Dutch cleanser, and waxed it.

I almost never saw her, but she said one day,
while I stood at her rushing downspout after rain,
how soft the water was. I didn't dare to touch.

Mr. Van Den Bosch, our landlord, who kept things straight,
put his plain and dull black bike in our garage
every night. His pants clips stared like giant spectacles,
black handcuffs, under the iron saddle. The bike
stood stiff, never leaned against our wood.

Bending into the splashes of sun and silver that time
I asked her, "Why do you save rainwater?"
and she said it made her hair soft.

Her long hair was graying, bunned back
tight, and no one ever went into that house
but me (once) and Mr. Van Den Bosch,
dismounting at 5:35 hunting things to fix.
She stole outside only once in a while for rain.

I would lie in the dark
to think there must be something near
to touch and feel the soft hair.

On Vacation, Teaching Bass

Listen, Bass,

Where is your self-respect?
I stood at your pond the last two dawns
under a dissonance of birds doing their bird-thing,
and I did my teacher-poet-at-leisure-thing, my fisherman-thing,
but you weren't doing your bass-thing at all.

I don't mind not existing; I understand about that;
I'm like anti-matter poking in, or God. Okay.
But the colors and whirrs that I pulled
through your world on transparent lines
were images, meant to do something, programmed through your genes
for millions of years.

Look. When you see that wounded wobble of red and white stripes
that I call a Daredevil lure, you're supposed to lunge
and strike — or at least get curious and follow.
but on casts and retrieves with just the right flash, vibration, and
        turning
I could see down there some thirty of you
shrug in your fishy way without the slightest shock of recognition.

Wake up! Have you no collective unconscious?
Take my Mepps Anglia #2 Spinner (which none of you did take):
it was assaulting two of your senses at once (not to mention your
        watery dreams),
it was 'the feel and body of the awareness that it presents' —
and there you stood, slowly waving pectoral fins,
as though you were trying to think, like pre-engineers.
A lure should not mean, but be!
The three of you dullards I did catch
went for fat, stock-response, mere-prosey worms.

One more thing. When I set my hook and get you on the line,
don't just go limp and come up unastonished.
You're supposed to seize the image and run with the line, tug
(I keep the drag on my reel set light; you can probably hear it sing),

run hard, break the skin between our two worlds, twist and shimmy in
    the air,
then arc and dive down deep. Keep tugging! That's your natural
    response, your instinct!

Next time we will talk about fly-casting,
maddening colors like stars on the top of your world.
Try to get yourselves open.

Bass dismissed.

Poem Beginning with a Line Memorized at School

Whither, indeed, *midst falling dew,*
Whither, Miss Pfisterer, black-dressed and balding
Teacher of English, lover of Bryant,
Whither did we all pursue
White glow the heavens with the last somethingsomething?

Bradley Lewis, I mean:
Who put aside with his cello and his brushes
Our lusty masculine sneers at his graceful ways,
Skipped the civics exam to father a son
And now designs engines with Mozart turned up loud.

Kenny Kruiter, I mean:
Expelled from high school for incantation with wine,
Who bends the knee to his common daily bread,
Hacks every day at bleeding sides of beef
And cheers twice a week the college basketball team.

Michael Slochak, I mean:
He always stuttered every dull thing he knew
And walked home alone — past home, to one gold period
When, crimson phrase against the darkly sky,
His jet purred into a green Korean hill.

Sisters, Daughters

My two older sisters went suddenly wide
in the hips, wore bandages called bras,
girdled down flat their bellies and butts.
There was a secretive hush through the house
like a sickly smell, something clamped tight
like their silken knees. I missed the ease
of the rabbits we had been, and
my father started taking me fishing.

You my three daughters all born dead
would now be growing round and sweet
and shy. I take your brother fishing.
He leaps through the brush at the shore
lean and swift as the tip of his flyrod.
He phones his girl every night. I look
at the curved river, missing you.

Seeing Pictures at the Elementary School

See
four yellow squash
waxing huge and plump
in the dark grass. Will they explode?
Grinning bees have lit the light green fuse.
The grass is dark. Juanita. Grade 2.

John's castle.
The drawbridge stretches asleep
over a moat of blue
where sailboats bob.
A smudge of black cannon aims at my face.
For all the flags and open doors
there is no road.

See the crooked lumpy dog
bark wide at the doghouse
because the doghouse growls
a rough purple NO
where a dog's name should be.
Roger, grade 3. See Roger bark.

My mind can't hear me talking this way.
This is not about art.
My mind is certain the lion is mean,

But Donna's lion gazes
through gauze of black
that drapes the bars
and the caption says,
the lion is mean
because children have closed the curtain.

Because I Never Learned the Names of Flowers

It is moonlight and white where
I slink away from my cat-quiet blue rubber truck
and motion myself to back it up to your ear.
I peel back the doors of the van and being
to hushload into your sleep
the whole damned botanical cargo of Spring.

Sleeper, I whisk you
Trivia and Illium, Sweet Peristalsis, Flowering Delirium.

Sprigs of Purple Persiflage and Lovers' Leap, slips of Hysteria
stick in my hair. I gather clumps of Timex,
handfuls of Buttertongues, Belly buttons, and Bluelets.

I come with Trailing Nebula, I come with Late-Blooming Paradox,
with Creeping Pyromania, Pink Appoplex, and Climbing Solar Plexus,
whispering: Needlenose, Juice Cup, Godstem, Nexus, Sex-us,
        Condominium.

Industrial Park

All this green hedging
going on: conduits snap and buzz underneath
and a cable just misses the goldfish
on its way to Plasticore, Inc.
Phoneline nerves sneak along roots
somewhere near the cutworms.

Pressure and voltage climb the network veins
and cascade up at the level of songbirds
and into white pavilions with popsicle windows
and tea-wafer roofs. Thousands stream in
through the turnstiles five days a week
to play, unwind, brief and debrief, eat lunch
industriously in the park on spreading music and carpet.
They touch the shiny equipment.

This is miles on the right side of the tracks
where packaged freight slips in and out at night like love
in long and glistening trucks.

So now and then I circle the Capital Beltway round and round
in the blue rubber truck,
dart into those parks from the night like a spark
and drop off under the stars and trees with love
    large oily gear wheels, hard maple sawdust,
    trainmen's lanterns, steam lunch-whistles —
and for use on alternate days
    rolls of pink tickets, striped picnic cloths,
    balloons and streamers, lemonade stands.

Davey Falling

On that day the boy shall come down at dusk
from the vacant hill, pulling his battered kite
over the ice-patched road, letting it scrape
and break. Behind the yellow
weeping windows of the kitchen
the soup shall whisper grace.
He shall smell his clean hands
and sit down between small songs his sisters.
Their forks shall chime together to ring the plates.
As easy as the blowing of steam from their cups
shall be the naming of the day's things.
His mother's fingers shall free a slow dance
in his shoulder-bone; his father's words
shall trust like the eyes of his English setter,
shall lay him down to sleep, and he
shall know, years later, always,
at any tugging of a line or string, shall know
that he had almost gotten home.

Four-Square Gospel

Old Uncle Fred could squint along forty-foot beams
And catch the gentlest wayward drift toward a curve
That no one else saw. His calloused, pitch-stained hands
Would tenderly stroke the flush seams of a perfect joint.
We used to see him astride his unwavering rafters,
Tall as the echoing blows of his worshipping arms,
Looking with pride on the loving work of his mitred,
Four-square world. He always looked sharply to see
If some sinning board in somebody's house were off square.
And longed to redeem it with the righteous tongue of his plane.

And then he slumped into arches and curves of age,
Propped up in a bed, looking out at the slanting east
While unseen termites encircled his squared-off house.
Puzzled, he eyed the long, sad arc of the geese,
The easy bend of a tree-limb heavy with fruit,
And then — we knew by the softening line of his mouth —
Saw the curve of a neck swinging free from the beams of a cross.

Walk the Edge

Get over the dunes and start along the shore
at sundown; bring big pockets, walk
not to go but to hoard
the cracks and grainings and lights
in driftwood and stones.

Make the walk spring or fall,
when few cottage lights up the dunes
can distract the drift
of your going or coming back. Drift.
Let it be down and into,
not along shore, that you go. Down.
Drift down

inside the spindrift
watch the wet edge for shapes
behind your eyes: fishes. Knots.
You can toss most shapes back
to the spendthrift Lake
for perfecting:

as deep as you are now
driftwood burns white in the dark
with time for wet sand to rub
the parent stars awake
against bone-touch of branches —
sandtime, slow as the turning of earth.

But that far is when to turn back.
You are almost too far in for love now,
almost out of time, turn now quick
to time, take breath to rise up,
you must get back, back up

to some landmark tree on a hill
can point you inland toward towns
and streets small but familiar,
the damp air of your room,

toward raucous morning
when grit of sandgrain in the sheets
and your heavy pockets
are almost strangers.

Letter to my son John, 1972

Letter from Home

At the Annapolis docks the yawl *Blue Puffin*
is for sale. So is the rough old skipjack
Grey Ghost. I buy

a plastic cup of worms,
drive Highway 2 five miles,
turn down that two-track road
trespassing past the signs that say I must not
to fish for perch. The point is

white sand below high pines
that cleaves Round Bay.
Since you and I took a wrong turn

blind into its lights, the point is
ours. Still
you haunt the plink
a sinker makes. And if you claim
what can't be bought

and forgive such roads the map won't tell —
then some time at that point
or if not then or there
in the twinkling of an eye
I'll see you, trespasser.

> *Letter to my son John (1955-1973)*
> *Written 1970; revised 7/31/73*

From *The Lost Faces* (1979)

I.

22nd Street, Holland, Michigan

The white houses brace their shoulders and stare
Like some hurt animal I once dreamed I killed
Who would not turn to beg or fight
But only stood and waited in the dusk.

I grew up here, want to call it home.
I never meant the swagger of the boy
Who hummed out happy over the county line
To play his luck out louder in distant towns.

Cradled on porches that hush to the whir of sprinklers,
The unmoved neighbors sip lemonade,
Never knowing me sick for home returning
To their new expressway, where I left the engine running.

Sidewalk Snowplows:
Holland, Michigan, in 1940

This must have been the last American town
to hire through snow
the shake of bells on the necks of horses.
Good morning began far out in the black
of barns, then lit up and sputtered into town
and jingled up the wind to our waking.
The snow didn't drop from dark or roofs
like the cold of sabbath bells
so much as it turned and rose like flakes
of horsey steam toward windows, ringing crystal.

Sometimes that sound was only the ching of glass
as a milkman struggled across the slippery yards —
but sometimes I could see in the frosty lights
a V-shaped sidewalk plow cut through, could hear
the snorting horse getting proverbed along
in Dutch by his redfaced farmer.
This is back in a time when everyone knew
the war would never come, back when children
were warned they should never give in
and lie down drowsy in blankets of snow.

Head Down

He disconnects the office intercom,
loosens his tie. His nose
works down the crook in his arm, flannel
sweet with his mother's washday soap,
down winters of corduroy steam
to the face of his sixth-grade teacher.
Drown out the Indian wars, shut off
the flow of exports from Madagascar
and Miss Kooman points her pointer
and says, "Put your head on the desk."

He can make enough dark with his hands
to let the drum beats in.
Through hemp and chocolate trees
he tracks the star-footed birds
out plains and canyons
scratched through the wood
where no one's allowed to write.
Before he raises again that treaty his face
into old clock-tick and new fluorescent hum,
he swears he will sometime carve his name
against the rules forever
deep in the top of the desk.

Second Commandment

Our church elders pinched a narrow view
of the sin of making graven images.
But the weather, loose catholic wench,
went right on making through the town
her shapes and trades of God.
I saw it sometimes in storms. Wet streets.

My Protestant Uncle Lyman took a chance:
from spaces behind his eyes he painted
my dead pioneer great-grandmother looking down
so we kids would know how real and kind
and rough and tender the angels look.
And then he made trees, and lights, and other faces.

The skate key under my shirt swung free
like the crucifix of some Irish tough
from the city thirty miles away
as gently the elders were graven one by one.

Conduction

"I want you always to remember this night,"
my father said. My mother lifted us
from bed. Madame Schumann-Heink was singing
on the radio, "the last time."
When I could open my eyes
to the bright Christmas lights,
my father was closing his to *Ave Maria.*
Sometimes his hand
would make little moves, conducting.

I remember the Gothic Philco,
the singer's name as distant as Europe.
Everything was being conducted
through sea waves. I remember
cocoa in a blue willow cup,
its Chinaman waving his hand to no one,
as though conducting. His air-waves
from far repeat from the little bridge
round and round the cup. My father's eyes
are blue. Schumann-Heink. Hands.
I do not remember the singing.

Missing Sleep

Slow down
sleep is not
the kind of train
you can run for,

remember
a crossing of tracks
with sand and still water
far back.

All your missed trains
set out
the steam and little bells
look for you

the wails and swinging
lights go out
to find you
at the old secret,

that foggy swamp
where there's
a rowboat
a boy you know

and ticking rails
half a mile short
of the boarded-up
hometown station.

X

Teacher's mark for a mistake,
X signs our teenage letters with a kiss,
then waits for us in gunsights up the road.

X is the sign all make who cannot make their names,
the picture children may not see,

the train which just might strike train Y
if we fail to solve the time for its space.

Turn your X in the air and bless yourself:
someone is marking a map in a rented room.
X is the stranger. Unknown quantity. Spy.
A half-wild light ray child-in-a-manger
shape to which we nail our fears.

Crossroad, crisis, crux, X is outrageous
crucifix brought bloody in through gates.

Sometimes when speech breaks down, we let
X mark the spot where our bombs will rain.

Or X is the little grave we won't forgive.
We drop to our knees in rage or worship. Come to X.

For L.P.

II. Children of Hamelin

Before He Heard of Hamelin

When feet walk the dark street
at night, that's a message
I try to hear. Or I watch
light happen
to startle the hair
of a child or a field of waves.
Sometimes news comes slower,
the swell of bread in the oven,

but either way, a slow and rising flight
or else the splinter
of thin in the wind
is why I flute.

Also because it wasn't just a dream
that I flew once
up from an afternoon nap
up sharp new light where I swung
from the railings and
high up the hole

the steps were running down
like scales below me.
In the hard square kitchen
I promised never again
to fly, but lied.

All trills and tootles now
I travel light. I patch my flappy
sleeves to taste like the smoke
of seasons: today tastes green,
tra-la. I can charm the very
squeaks and thrashings behind the walls
into space that's still.

The next town, Hamelin,
I never heard of. It calls.
Don't call me back.
Or call me.
I like the sound of the wind.

Overheard about Mr. Bunting

(Several children of Hamelin speak:)

The rags he flies from his coat
are a torn-up flag.
I don't know what country. It's old.

The first time
I wanted to run
under my bed.
I had forgotten sizes.

The only thing I remember like this
is my father whispering long ago
that his back-ache came from sleeping in trees.

I dreamt the bridge fell in
and we were like fish
who watched, surprised,
and I thought about Mr. Bunting.

Well, he was anyway
all make-believe
so I ran to him
and when I got there
he was there.

If my mother saw him at night
she would tell him to turn down the lights.

Every patch
in his coat
is a lit-up place
across a river.

Coming Back Down to Hamelin

(June 20, 1284: Having drowned the rats,
he has been thrown out without pay as a
drunken sorcerer, but now he decides to return.)

Who could be angry up here?
This path spills happy
drunk in stoney streams
cold and blue to my feet.
The rain or the wine is melting
the mountain, rocks up here
go round to boulders. Faces
can change. These hums in my head
and Saint Francis talking to birds
and my pipe are for people to catch.
So forgive them. Corkscrew back
to the road, uncertain why,
down to that crooked town
and make it dance.

Windy Night in Hamelin

(The Pied Piper speaks:)

To children I'm glow coals of wool
or a tall glass of milk in moonlight,
it depends on the weather.
From one of their houses
a door knob rises over a bush and shines;
my patched coat is cathedral windows,
dogs no longer bark at me.
God bless the air!
The wrinkled colors it shakes.

The cloth merchant's son
has his father's eyes that steal
and I want to bring
strong dark grain from the mountains
but the lights at their table are bright.
That dark woman who hobbles
knocking her cane at a cat
used to stretch out in grass.
I step around the space

of a boy who died.
In my town, if you kicked a flower
you had to pay a just fine.
I kick these clowning leaves
that scratch like sparks and goodbyes,
shuffle a rising dance —
then wonder where the wind goes.
My children you are flying out
and I am trying to follow.

The Notes He Left

Hamelin
June 26
Year of Our Lord 1284
Sunrise   no breeze

The question is not silver
but what's in the air.

Somedays the wind will whine
around corners and windows, restless.

When there are no breaths in the air
you try to hear them.

The rats that sank — were they
the souls of the parents?

I have heard of such things.

Near the end of stillness, there's always
this light whistle through grass

before the rustling
of leaves and wings

and I know that sharp note which the breaths
blow over the hole in the world.

The Hamelin Epilogue

(1) *Hamelin Decree*

That the gate through which they passed
      shall bear a plaque,
As shall the Calvary Mountain which swallowed them.
That the story shall be painted in windows and churches.

That after the date set down of the year of Our Lord
All public documents of the town shall add
The date of the year of the going-forth of the children
Thus: *Anno liberorum suorum exitus.*

That no drum, pipe, or musical instrument
Of any kind shall henceforth sound in the street
Leading to the gate through which they passed.
That no tavern be there, nor any joy.

(2) *Needing a Better Word*

(1286: A citizen of Hamelin writes:)

Anno Secundo liberorum suorum exitus.

Children is cold and hollow, a lamentation
of ice and wind. The sound is reprimand,
chapped skin, collisions muffled in snow.

Maybe we should call them *startles.*
A girl is not as bright as a *flicka;*
chil and *dren* miss all but darkness and bone.

I need some winking word for my own young —
but six of my startles sleep in the ground
stubbornly *children* no matter how I call them

and call them, and winter coming on.

(3) *The Piper Still*

. . . a world they can live in.

Not here,
these biting needles of light.
Like any old ghost
I refract to silence
bend down easy
to cracks between keys. And I wait.

III.

Chickens

They stagger off balance, hugging
wings that won't fly. Air
is a stranger's hand to their feathers.
Lidless eyes stuck open,
they reel in and out
earth-tight and cockeyed
through lights that won't go out
till wind is the only dark they know.
Broody for all their dead eggs,
they prawk and gargle dry
through stones, scratch down yards
and yards of the earth.
All night in the brooders, electric
nightmare eggs glare down.
Inside the plastic meat
pumping steroids glow like dying
stars, shoot through entrails
that have nothing portentous to say.

If they could only breed and brood
in some dark
sensing shadows
and what to drift back to
they'd know again to fly
their folded arms.
I throw the dumbclucks some skins
from their scuppernong vine
they cannot fly into or climb
and decide I'll fox in some night.
In a wicker basket I'll gather
their lightbulbs, pour scuppernong
wine in their mash,
and the next morning pluck them
from swaying and singing
high in live oaks.

Potatoes

. . . the scarcely innocent underground
stem of one of a tribe set aside for evil.

                                        Ruskin

The tribe is deadly nightshade,
"used to relax eye muscles" and
to kill. Akin to the bittersweet
we used to strip and hang by its feet
in the dark basement
until it cracked its yellow lids
and wrinkled open red.

Potatoes yawn in that dark. Pale wet
sprouts spill out of eyes
as though the dark had sprung a leak.
Once I secretly shoveled into the furnace
my father's boot, bulging with their stems.
They'll crawl all night blue-veined
toward stairs, toward us.

Cut out their starry eyes
and fling them into black, each one
will beam a limp and stemming eye
back toward light — not to break free
but to blink and catch
the old rhythms that pump potatoes,
innards hugely white in the dark —

feeding 400 years of history,
steaming hills, "enough to feed an army."

Early Coffee

Hair and nails grow in the dark;
all night the spiders spin
lines to catch the blue buzz,
pulsing, hum of words
through cells that sleep.
To drowse before dawn is to net
the spin and stretch of things
that darkly grow
as the world tips and falls to light.

The sky has torn its hangnail red.
Through bark and twist of twigs
the morning moves like a herd of steer,
rising stiff from roads. It steams.
Cars begin to stream the freeways,
wide-eyed yellow current down wires.
In breaking light I try to hold
the dark nest that's cupped in my hands.

Wanting Supper

There should be fog horns down below
the street. Blown scraps of faces
that won't look up. A clutching of collars.
He had slammed the kitchen door when he stomped out.
Gray awnings should cry all over the dirty
faces of stores. Let there be lightbulbs
hanging dim from single cords
and foreign shopkeepers glaring down
the blue flues of his eyes to the hole
in his pocket. I'll bet she's sorry now,
he thinks: he smells like a sheep, his oldest coat
is gaping loose at a seam, and no one
asks what he wants. He wants dark halls
of garlic over the shops, an indignation
of thin soup for supper. He wants to cry.
The city should drag its feet like the word *because,*
it should be raining black as explanations.

But it's only an evening sprinkle in May, soft
in the suburbs. The student clerk in the all-night store
knows him, sends an unwanted smile from the shine
of plastic wrappers. He buys a quart of vanilla.
Back in the street he picks up some wino's bottle
wrapped in a twisted paper bag; he holds it
under the street light, but no one is looking.
He brings it to the green receptacle,
thinking, *Well, maybe she's punished enough.*
He says hello to a kid from Sunnyside Drive.
Things are losing all their strangeness again.
He turns back toward home, six blocks away,
certain by now the dining room chairs have changed
beyond the memory of dinner.

Lovers' Quarrel

She has trudged down to where he works
And sees him stand too narrow, too close
   For love to what he builds,
Tight on his scaffold in a shaft of shade.
   His back muscles have shrunken
Since morning; his saw rips short jerks.

Careless of her skirt, she stoops
To smooth a white cloth and spread his lunch
   In sunlight and yellow leaves.
When he sees her she is leaning forward
   Easy, long arms loose
As her hair which is blowing across her mouth.

Although he straightens, he does not come down.
His head nods *no* with the words they exchange.
   Past glint of plum and bottle-
Green she darts home through leaves,
   Her back feeling his eyes
And warm with the long, loose strokes of his saw.

A Gruntled Poem for Greeting
a Feckfull and Wieldy Day

All things are down and doing
so commonly green and quick
that I give this clement day
my swerving love.
I sniff and watch in dogged ease
gainly girls at the corner bus-stop
so fretless and seemly
they could be gathering to pluck
dulcet grapes from slopes.
Of all the unmitigated sweet!

This old boyhandled world
picks me down
to such a perfect flation
that I can't uncorporate.
I drag my formity
amuck this alloyed happiness.
Hand me, villain!
my mind is coming hinged.
With bending determination
I earth my old flesh of contention

and shuffle soft-shoed into death
with all deliberate torpor.

The Shore of the Sky

Sleep with me on the beach.
Our sails will flap back and forth
and touch so lightly
we do not feel water
lapping the ribs
of the washed-out hull we become.
Inside it a red lantern rubs
and slowly swings.
Shooting stars fall down
the tunnels behind our eyes
and hold their matches
still enough
to light up colored birds
and fish on the walls.
We keep waking up
less awake each time
but wide alive to the sky:
we peer up from this long
low field of stargrains
into handfuls of
beach sand hanging high.

Early Morning Exercise, Lake Michigan*

White sands under my feet rub and crunch
and whistle against themselves. I lay their little notes
under my footprints — put them back to bed.
Like any shipwreckful of drowsiness
and breath, I can softly be taken in
by this treachery of muffled diminuendo.
Some time I'll beach myself where the music stops.

Not now. Day breaks open with gab of gulls
while dunegrass holds C-sharp above the watercrash.
I try again to discover my feet.
This rushed cacophony beating up the surf
may be the world's last jazz band shaking loose:

Listen: that clarinet is curling
green and tart its thin-lipped gripe
around hot brass that pushes it, and now
they make the sap leap up and hit the light
that plumps the blue grapes up the dunes.

*In 1946, the National Association of Teachers of Speech voted on the ten
worst-sounding words in English. Seven of them are *cacophony, crunch, gripe,
jazz, plump, sap,* and *treachery.*

Fresh Fruit for Breakfast

All night we were softly tangled in the sky's
vineyard of small white grapes

now that much more than the seven flavors of Jello
shake their covers from orchards and hills

o let the children's wild shouts upstairs
steal our dark thunder of hallelujahs

let fruitstains on their mouths be psalms
kissing hello the seventy thousand tons of light

that fleshed the dark this year, rejoicing
in juice of these berries, peaches, plums.

The Work of Our Hands

He would come home tired at night from making things,
his hands still dreaming the prints of handles:
my *pakke*, great-grandfather, maker of windmills
       in Friesland.

Out of the wind, he would probably stare at his fire.
The work could go on alone, sails and beams
angled to translate every pull and push of wind
to the balance of brake-wheel.
While hand-cut spur gears rhyme the shaft,

his shapes could turn in drowsy in his head.
Only the hands remember a good day's work:
it's like falling asleep with your bride,
or fishing in the dark after the fish have stopped
but you think you feel them still through the hand.

I know that space. Though my *pakke* died before
       I was born,
carving ornate balustrades in Chicago mansions,
I finally fished and sailed and felt the wind and bought
a sail and now I know that throb in my hand.

The gift is tension, drag. I'll never wish again
to feel the sail rise up from the water and soar
toward the thrill and loop of a hollow scream:
even birds when they sing grip their hands down hard
into bark that is rooted and cuts the wind.

My hands hug shape. The prow leaps down for more.
Pakke, I write and sail as a displaced,
       unemployed millwright.

Imagining Wieger Jellema (d. 1894)
For William Harry Jellema

Heading In

Night breeze stirs the hair on my arm.
I hear trees moving along the shore.
The mast of my little boat
plots arcs and points in the dark,
uncertain. She bobs no light.

My son and I all day have reaped the wind
and made the daggerboard tick
as we cut through sunlight and breakers.
His hands are quick to tiller and line.

White stars bloom soft down this desert of water.
Only my hands remember the day.
Each slow flap of sail is an ache in the arms.
I wish all boats had still a man's work,
could bring something back.

I am not quite lost in these reflections of stars.
Pakke's old cells call through my bones
to say, "You are losing your son,"
but a neighbor's light on the dune points home.

Some night as he sails here alone
my son will pick up and bring back
senses the mind can never know about wind,
his past, work, losses, his hands.

For John
Fragment, 1972

Going to Work at Yaddo

At the artists' colony
I leave the mansion
and walk to work early
across frozen grass
in old shoes and jacket.
I see through breath
the hard stones.
Dark pines are watching.
Thermos under my arm,
I swagger,
swing the black lunchpail,
old emblem of manhood,
whistle each day
different tunes
from the thirties.

Child awakened
by footsteps and
factory whistle
I watch through frosted glass
a whistling man
stride off to work.
Just before
his key makes touch
with the

studio door
he looks about
the empty woods.
I am not there.

Touching It

(1) *Snow*

I have drowsed in and out of four naps.
The first snow, falling all day outside,
makes fur of any good room.
While in dreams I was trying to find
four little things I had lost,
the snow was piling high
and drifting the sills, the road.
Swirls of woolgathered white:
I close my eyes and shake, and down it comes.

It covers anything. I have forgotten
all but the shapes
of lost things in the dreams.
The late-summer death of son John
gets deep and in place, like the car
out there on the road, drifting in snow.

(2) *Glass*

I found beach sand in a pocket
this coldest day of the winter —
he would have liked those pulverized
stars, rising from valleys
inside the jeans
and reflecting a hot
lightbulb in the closet.

But he would throw the stars away
as I just did,
brushing them off.

*What are you going to be
when you grow up?*
I ask my aging face in the glass.
I always ask, but with the tap

I make quick clouds of steam,
the crystal ball is clouded,
no answer but a wink and a young
cocked grin which fogs over.

(3) *Walk*

This broken stone
says I'll get my finger on you
so gently
you'll stir up and kick with me through sand
like a friend

mortal and afraid
surprised to have someone along
as cool as you
you shivering old bastard
death.

(4) *Survivor*

My youngest son has put in his cap
the good stones,
the ones he believes in.
He is out in the breakers.

I bow down before stone:
a glazed one ordains me
to be its thin streak
of red mouth.

I'm an old stone. Cool.
The spark is in deep.
Now I can start to talk
to the tips of his fingers.

1974

Fishing over Shipwrecks,
I Catch the Word *Spectral*

Bells of lost ships
ting as they graze
dark valleys of seaweed.
They follow each other
down the distance of rust.
Wait to be heard.

I touch that world deep
with a tremble of thin
fishing line.
Their blind towns wait
for the holds to break.
Learn to let go.

Down there they see line
off the reel of a star
slanting through water.
It ignites the spectral
scales of a fish.
Look up and stay down.

The red of my lure
once waited in black.
Then it scratched
through its fur
and started to glow.
Praise mother dark.

Report from Near the End of Time and Matter

If only we could see for a moment
the holy light we pursue. . . .

                    Plotinus

Say it is now the third month of light.
Your eyes can't filter it out. Try
to tuck your head under your blazing arm,
try to find the sloping back to shade.
Out along the flat plane of your gaze
no aura from tree can print itself on your eye.
Remember colors? Thick and cool. Old saints
in glassy rag and skin who hung
between us and the Sunday sun. But now
nothing shines in this total bright.
There is no shadow flickering in a window,
no dark in which to remember depth. Even
the blood shade of your eyelid is clearing to white.

Cutting Paper with Matisse

Drawing with his scissors, one whole movement
linking "line with color, contour with surface,"
Henri Matisse must have left an awful clutter.
To find those scraps of color now
from which he lifted shapes would be to find
strange negatives of paintings,
the stencils of the firmament.
Perhaps it only happened while cleaning up
that he picked scraps off the floor
and pasted them onto their positives
like pieces of the mirrors
in which his mind was learning to see.
The eyes can never see enough.
He cut his random way through stacks of paper,
even sailed to Polynesia just to study
"the altered proportions of light and space."

This random poem of mine has nothing to study at all;
it follows a child's left hand
strolling a right-handed scissors
through silent planes of snow
to anything. To the stiff paper snowflakes
I tried one day to cut in my room after school,
all geometric, little chops and snips.
To the magnified snowflakes I studied later,
swirling our valleys. Through microscopes
I saw fields rinsed by stains of gentian violet
to colors blazing in from every side
and still those shapes, and other shapes that
the dreamer hand remembers and remakes

until the sea is churning spirochetes
and fossil-leaves, tiny bird wings from back
so far behind the lens that only the hand can find them,
and moons, and the sky holds still to show
protozoa orbiting the little bones of fish.

Matisse: The Cut-outs, National Gallery of Art, October 1977

Hibernation

Is there still white?
I can hear through this dark fat
the rub I left with a tree
when there was green.
Its roots hold the hum
in their hairs.
Down the cave behind my eyes
I almost see nearly berries.
First comes the bright ache picture
of water, then circles of colors
I swim through, shapes of juices.
And then I'll remember the rest.
To wake will be hungry and hard.

Ancient Instruments

The piano is indirect.
Her fingers aren't touching the tense nerves of a lute.
Through mechanical levers they translate
        to hammers and pads
that press constructed chords.

She wants music to sound
the hums the ancients made strange lyrics for
so they could catch the words of the
        gods. Who won't return.
Deeper still she listens

to windchimes: music moves
off what the wind will make of scales just hung there,
random bonesticks strung from narrow wires.
        When wind
reels in as blind as a cave,

deaf as stone to the notes
it harps upon, the tones in her willow tree
can pick a prayer of hollow bones that says again
where all the music starts.

First Climb Up Three Surfers' Peak

(A dune at Lost Valley, on Lake Michigan,
named in memory of John Jellema, Todd Eaddy,
and Bill Smalligan — d. 1973)

"Tell the vision to no man." (Matt. 17:9)

After we drove three stakes and nailed
the wooden sign *Three Surfers' Peak*
into its foot, I climbed
the dune, stood up to
its wind on the razorback edge
to watch and wait.

      No sign.
No countenance shone upon me.
I could not get blinded by light
of the sand, and surf.
Although the waves and the beach
got small, there was no Transfiguration.
The three memorial boys didn't show,
nothing did, although I swore to god
I would have left them once again
and come back down
from that forbidden place
to hunks and beating colors,
watercrash, the timid dartings of deer
into long grass, cry of a child
and all the empty corners — back to
these tangled things they knew.
I swore like Jesus
I'd work back down to love
and the faces in streets,
but I knew this note I was leaving
could be the lie
on which to twist my way up
to the light
an hour before I climbed the peak
so no one would know what happened
just in case it did.

From *The Eighth Day:*
Poems New and Selected (1984)

I.

From Trout Run: A Poem in Seven Movements

(3) Stranger in the Village

Walking, my friends here insist, is good: it smokes the scotch.
I walk the streets of Trout Run in the lurid disguise
of the Stranger. A schoolboy on a bike rides next to me
and asks where I'm going. *Oh, just walking,* I say,
just walking all over the streets of this old town.
He does not believe me. So now I have him:
now whatever truth I say offhand will be to him

some flash of legend. He asks me where I'm from.
I shrug. *From fairly far away,* I say: *Just came in
from Michigan* — and I hook my thumb over the mountains, west.
He winks and grins as though I've told him Pluto.
Now we are friends. *How far are you going?*
Oh, just to the end of some final street, then back —

and now, like a boy encountering some made Jesus
but trusting, he suddenly stops his weaving bike.
Who are you? he asks. That question older than fire
for which I am never ready. To what can I witness?
I am the piper without a pipe, Adam looking for home —
all this truth tricks me to say I'm a poet — as though
that's still a job. And then the boy reaches back
for some tribal voice as old at least as his mountains.
He hooks his thumb toward the end of the street.
At the hotel, he says, *they'd probably give you a beer, for free.*

Application

What is your permanent address?

> The wind through Thick Street
> hasn't settled down.
>
> Look for me in words like *startle, plum.*
> They may have to forward you back to *dark*
>
> unless I hit the blue and lonely town
> whose little lights I almost glimpse
> whenever somebody blesses me when I sneeze.

What memberships do you have?

> I belong to those who remember
> and seldom say
> who don't join up with much.
>
> Member. I think I'm a carpal
> just left of the spike
> in the left hand of Jesus.

Briefly describe the obstacles to your work:

> Eve.
> No left turn.
> That God made sweet sunfish
> so full of bones.
> Forgetting.
> Remembering
> it isn't Eve.

Describe the audience you wish to reach with this project.

> Far off
> in yellow kitchens after supper
> they wonder if it's the trees
> in the wind or the wind in the trees
> and they are really listening for stones.

What other means of support do you have?

The stick.
Forgiveness.

The speech of any child
who rejects its dying out,

any star out there that lights on straw
instead of pointing only
yet another star out there.

When do you expect to finish?

Perhaps at hearing my name
just when I know I no longer need
that saddest of words, the word *because*

perhaps some warm afternoon
between the rise of a sailing breeze
and the far ring of a phone
smell of apples halfway up
a thought about my hand.

Two Sleepless Men

If you've ever worked in the building trades,
you know how you almost get used to the hammers
that knock asleep through dust and wind
of hallways as long as night. But just
beneath those beats you feel your fear
of slipping off rafters and thrilling down through the ribs.

Maybe long ago some carpenter
new to the trade went back to the job
one night — let's say for his lunchpail —
and found between the studs
nine moons skating in drops of water
over its black enamel — and possibly shadows
of willow dancing through the bonework —
and maybe he joined them — what if he did? —

so maybe that's who's prowling tonight,
keeping you awake: some workman,
not thieving or lost, but back to visit
your long-since settled neighborhood.
Confused by thick and paint and how
the trees have grown, I'm looking for something.
You'll help if you turn out your light.

After Looking Long at His Pictures of the Civil War, Having First Dropped a Chocolate Peanut Butter Pie Upside Down on His Georgia Carpet, I Dream of Zimmer

Water is brown and yellow-brown smoke lies low
in marsh grass. Inhaling. There goes I think
my Uncle Ben with those other baggy soldiers
trudging through sepia brown. Horses tug at caissons
and soldiers slog. They wave to the camera that's taking
these blown-up moving 3-D pictures of World War I
and I totter on the edge of the frames and feel the suck

dizzy until I fall in. I rise, march with a group, fall
in step or try to fall in step, skip to adjust,
use the soldier on my left for a pacer —
but he gets tangled down, stumbles, skips-to-
adjust but trips and hesitates *(yer left, yer left)*
and looks at me for help and it is Zimmer!
We laugh. As backpacks slip and clunk and splat
we hug, then limp off in broken step with each other.
What place is this, I ask, what regiment, which war?

"The peasants have plenty for supper," Zimmer says.
He squints ahead. "We are the klutzes of World War I,
the Losers, hand-picked by the Army for Zeppelin school."
Knowingly we laugh again hard, we hoot and hitch the muddy
tackle up and keep sloshing ahead. Left-footed rookies
in a lost battalion, headed not at all toward
any front, we wade through 1918 happily
toward unsuccess and our era, our distant births,
sensing how baffled those shy girls our mothers will be.

A Word in the Glare

"Few of the blind are mad," Roethke told his journal —
then wagered his mind by leaping with open eyes
down the shafts of power into halls of light.
And Edward Hopper took his life to paint
the terrible proportion of light to emptiness,
a final room containing nothing else, and full of it.
What we can't help staring into is not just the invisible
presence of God, but also His visible absence.

This is not an age of dark, but of glare.
The Scriptures warn of it: woe unto them
that put darkness for light, and light for darkness.
Woe to them that deflect us from signs and dreams
to the lighted streets and squares of authorized lives.

These complex pictures force the imagination
back to thing, and back to so simple a thing as a word.
I want now simply to bring in hand the light and dark
of one of the single words for which I grieve: Treblinka.
It makes three winks, a petticoat, tremble of bell
of silver, then magic light forever charred like chimneys
stuck in the throat of history: Treblinka.
Though there's not enough dark to show it, the candle I've lit
shakes for a lunatic word I do not want to say: Treblinka.

Dawn Train through Valparaiso

The year the Civil War turned back to sleep,
some Latinate dream of Paradise Valley stirred
here in Indiana, lost amid alien corn.
In the mercy of dark I can turn this Valparaiso into
the one in Chile, where I have never been: tangled flowers
up mountainside suburbs and over those Andes
the way Neruda once fled, an outlaw with a disguised
bundle of poems and two good bottles of wine.
But in these streets, in the flashing light of Blatz, Blatz,
no one will hunt you down for subverting the system
with poems. They will never take notice. Here they make
tankcars full of paint and Lutheran college degrees.
Dante makes pizza. The truckers from Gary
and Chi call this place Valpo, plain as motor oil.
The downtown houses are teeth in rusty gears.

In the dark train window I try to remember my face
fifteen years before this passing through: lecturer
with a breaking life who came to Valpo U. like a truck to pronounce
the end of Christian Humanism. Weak research but right
perception, that untyped conference paper lies still
with half my life in a box marked "to be filed." I know again,
clean through my dusty face to the squeal of signal lights,
that "four hundred years of humanist faith in man
leave us longing for half-remembered places, for miraculous rain."

Here comes the light. Indiana has nowhere to hide.
It didn't really have the time to nurture a cathedral
out of these broken plains. What is missing is not
the skyward shot that's dizzy swaying off the tips
of spires, what we ache for is the weight
of hewn stone holding down here, grave
with us through glare or night, silent
yet huge with mass to wait with us
for some end that could bring us round.

The train is running out of town
to mourn. It picks up speed.

Far on the edge, in an old frame house,
a muffled light in an upstairs room
says someone is sick, or dying.
We are hurtling past someone's end,
no one knows how to stop,
get off this train. God's priest for now,
obsolete as the pre-dawn train for Chicago
that no longer stops, I mumble remotely
the Latin I never learned: *pace, misere,*
mea maxima culpa. I make Christ's furious sign
with a fist where the dinning bell
tears open red in the dark near the end
at the dangerous crossing.

Crab Cactus

Deformed and staunched like the stump
of a claw, it hunches toward light.
The stalk that it is accumulates
its fleshy lack of decency
time out of mind in the sands.

Eons ago it sulked itself pale
and fled the cool shadows of Eden,
sure that the spoken *it is good*
of Genesis could not apply.
Now an old exile and hardly
a plant, it sucks the air
like a stone and does not cry out.

But late each December for just one night
it forgets the feud. Mad as a magus
it brings between spikes one bloom
of outcast star, God only knows
to whom from where or why.

After the Frisian of Fedde Schurer, 1898-1968

Wire Triangulations

In the second layer of the city they called "New York"
almost no objects survived intact
but our teams did find in white ashes
more than twelve million triangular wire sculptures
each with a curved hook protruding from its apex.
These shapes were almost certainly objects of worship:
most are found in small dark windowless rooms
which are often named with a derivative of their verb
to close, meaning to end, and also of their word for intimate.

We do not yet know why these protected
and almost indestructible wire triangulations
were so numerous among the occupants of the World
that Killed Itself, or just how they link to the violent
fascination these people had with destruction and death.
The precise meaning and function of these probable gods
will surely be found in our investigation
into the meaning of triads in their religion and into *hanger* —
a word from which our computers will surely uncover a verb.

Letter to Myra Sklarew, Visiting Mekounida, on the Island of Evvoia, in Greece

Lost Valley
Montague, Michigan
July 7, 1982

Dear Myra, in one of the fifteen houses of that high village
you need: by now you would join the lamentation
of ancient women sighing dark as shawls
to think I had sent the postman and his donkey
struggling up that dusty mountain path
from the little harbor at Karystos all the way up
only to say *how are you I am fine we miss you here.*

This must be worth his hire. I pray to God the ding
of goatbells and a closer hum of bees in thyme
will make light of the road this note must go.
I pray for the donkey's feet, for three faithful hands
at least that will cross the postman a blessing,
for cold water up the way that tastes of stone,
for a breeze and a hush of wine back down to Karystos.

And now it feels so ancient and good to pray aloud
like a peasant I also pray for rain to lay quick hands
on dust, for the strong green breath of onions in high fields.
Peace to the sheep who graze in rocks. May olive trees
push thick and heavy up the tilted yards and groves,
let lutes tonight and sleep twine deep as candlelight
in vines, Lord make the cheese turn gently in the crocks.

From the Great Lakes I have only small news: our swamp that went
almost dry behind the dune is back this year. Down here
the bullfrogs snap their banjo strings all night, and crickets twitch.
Machines knocked down the oldest house in town, the blacksmith's
    shop.
We're meeting in the small white church to try to stop the bomb.
At dawn just after a storm, near the shore, I saw a scarlet tanager
ignite black pine — this high priest without camouflage who still
survives in light. But what I must tell you most: I saw
the way light leans into the greenstain side of a shipwrecked beam

and it made me feel something about the weather
of which a nervous laugh is only a modern translation.
The moon had been eclipsed, there had been that storm, and then
this other light, this almost microscopic whelming. Something is
    wrong.
Tell me if you feel the trembling there above Karystos. Love.

Letter from Friesland to My Sons

Fear burns its lights late in America's night
    and I'm not there. Up here in Friesland
learning to read the surviving sounds our ancestors made,
    I have cut the electric din of English.
It is like a vow of silence. Deprived of the insight of speech,
    I only hear as echo some far and ancient music.
Forgive me. I have chosen for now to be dumb.

This flat land I try to claim is a tiny forever;
    the four towns I can name through my window
are only the middle distance — the eye goes on and on
    swimming the slow flow of canals.
The cobbled roads, unimpeded by hills, graze slowly as sorrow
    beside the still water that always returns.
The seasons stay, they doze lightly as ages beneath each other —

there are no junctures, time circulates like a heaviness
    in speech, like village smiles, like sun
and nitrates churning through cows and grass. A seamless world.
    So I think I remember from centuries ago
these Frisian faces, and I know I've heard before tonight

this stormy wind, the thumps and shouts of an angry preacher
    wing collar askew as he breaks
his diphthongs against indifferent roofs and branches and stars.
    And the calm is familiar, too: the way
consonants soften and wash like tides, and never tick.

Adrift like a child drowsy in church who wants to make
    a world in the smell of his mother's fur,
I try to make from this beginning, before the end
    of our sweet good time on the earth, just once,
images that turn on themselves and echo ahead, out of time.
    Mute but only partially deaf,
I write notes for now on the third side of the page.

I'll come back, of course, but back each time some small part short
    of the whole way back to where you grow.

So listen: old Frisians say what to do about mystery and loss,
   about all the unspeakable beauty and grief:
if it can't be said, a Dokkum proverb goes, *then you must sing it.*
   I'm learning. Forgive me. I want to have words
with you tonight, but the canal going back has no translation.

A Double Contention against the Scriptures

I don't understand how the old lament
There is no new thing under the sun
can be true. I see
new things. A schoolgirl showed me
a painting she made today

and now I have this picture
in my head, surely it's new,
of ghosts as wavey lines of light
that try to thicken to colors

so they can form and come back.
The girl said dew is the tears
the dead people leave on the grass
when they can't quite make it home.

That's new. So is the thought I got
that now every stir
of shadow through air
craves having a body

and these things ache alive
like the newly closing space
left by your son
I try to forget

who died last week. I remember
Let not the sun go down upon thy wrath
but tonight that miser
same old penny sun
slid down again red on my wrath.

For the parents of Gus

Flieger's Barn

Inside the hot green smolder
of unripe straw, the *ching*
of the scythe waits under rust.
In its dark chapel the bell
of the summer cow is still
but it summons anyway the rising
steam from a pail of milk
sweaters of high school girls
the heave and fall of lamps
that sway under storms
and startle wings and dust
high up the hoots of rafters.

Red mouth of a woman is what
the poem was moving toward
when it started out,
and butter pressing through
the seams like light —
but it forgot to invent
a road going back.
By now dark owns the barn
but rents it out some nights
to the moon. Inside and out
the red barn beats and flags
from the far-off snow.

To the Man in Room 321

You asked how it was when I got lost
from the bus and the others
and stumbled into Frazzleburg, Maryland,
and tore my dress. I'm glad somebody asked.
Frazzleburg looked tired. Shredded brick houses
snarled on the edge of grumpy sidewalks.
Its hair was standing on end.
The mailman hobbled in a hemp overcoat
up and down the shocks and frowns of porches.
A rusty truck chugged alone
on an unstitched sidestreet, grinding its teeth.
But say don't I seem to remember something
didn't we live there once, me just down
the hairpin turn of Muzzle St. from you
in the white exhaust at the corner of Cock?
Why yes I think I can see you now
ripping the sacks of gorse and furze and fratch
with sharp fingernails. You were bigger then.
Was that you? Was that me? I see
why you asked about my trip, it's nice
to relive those good old days that fade away.

The Weather Is Always Good

Changes of weather curl inside
and wait to resound. Sometimes
grief stretches out in our eyes,
lies tight and thickens the tissue
until the lights coming in are dim.
Its wind is black and still.
And even this is seasoning, fresh

and right until curtains flutter inward
and grief plays light
through trembling poplars, light
in a net of mist on the lake
that we watch thoughtless and mute.
From the stir of internal murmur we say
how impossibly bright these things are.

After a Macedonian poem by Aco Šopov

Just Breathe

You and that coming breath
have been through thin together.
It arrives with its little hands
full of drift and absence
toward something like home.
A shutter claps in the wind.
Beneath the beats of the heart
that murmur *be* and *be,*
air takes the shape of a wing
and every thing catches its weight.

Just breathe. In and out.
The next wave startles the next:
the snow will rearrange
its drifts along the fence,
sailcloth will belly and luff
as the breeze swings to the south.
Anything else that's part
of the rhythm will follow:
breathe again, loosen, dip,
lean on the dancing.

Beyond where breath disappears
far over your shoulder, stars
refuse to take note, they go only
out and out. But never mind.
Everything sings to a gentle
raising and drawing of blinds
and a turning up and down of lights.
For all its domesticity,
the next breath is the wildest
rumor of angels you know.

White on White

Just in from the snow, my mind
is the white road out there
filling in as it died behind me
all the way home. Perhaps
as it lost its way in and out
it ran out of one kind of time.

I shake and brush my coat
and lashes and stomp my feet
but something is not going to leave.
The white star lights
I may once have steered by
still fall down streets
and lawns and down behind my eyes,
down optic caves, like galaxies
receding into a rim of space.
White has followed me home from the snow.

I listen here behind the door in the dark:
nothing up the sky is so far out
that its soundings cannot resonate
the stillest mind: and now I know deep
that the white in my yard is not still:
its mass is energy, it lies
like the black holes implicit for years
in Einstein's abstract equation
lying there quiet on paper. I hold on
tight along an icy curve of thought:

That there's some eighth day of the week
inside the window reflection that jumps
into place as I flick on the light: there
for a second my brown coat is raining, my hood
is still tied, the monk I was is humming soft
as candleflame to a white figure rising from white.

Meditation on Coming Out of a Matinee

I try to trust the light
before I step off into it.
I think death is not dark,
I know my fear of the light.
Death is more light than I can think.

I've seen what death feels like:
I woke one morning to light from
beyond the white curtain
but the lamps in the room still on
bright as if it's already night.

Yes, like that.

The Self Trying to Leave the Body That It Is

You're all skin the rough heat of sumac
thickened with bruises. Body, you pant
rank steam while onions eat our breath.
You're itch, you're a grind of sockets,
you're meat that sags and jerks in turn.
Why do I think of sour cabbage clubbed
purple and drying in halls? Don't answer:
if I let you speak for yourself
you'll chug and saw like oldtime Sunday
in a wooden church, all maroon and black,
far from the yellow mercy of blowing wheat.
You want me under your skin — I want

to fly light and not remember pull, wing.
Just go away. Go knock me some possible
door through your cells. I'll rise
some hollow way. Out distant fields
I yearn to see the brassy fat bells
stretch thin into harpstrings, hairs,
auras, until they pale into strands
of wind over snowfields, whispers of cold.
Old lover, drag and heft, why can't you
let me break out? Take heart: I've crossed
our arms like this over our chest so we
can separate in the dignity of a sign.

On Edge

Be grateful to the gunman
who inches the shade aside
to pin you on the fine lines
of his cross. Give thanks to the wild
night of dogs gone mad, or rising ice,
thanks to the drunk who weaves
his bleary headlights cold across
the hairs on the back of your neck.
Bless the man's knuckles that whiten around
a length of pipe, empty freight cars standing
in snow, bless light from the mortuary.
Hum in the dark to the halting
knock of your heart on the door of its cave,
sing praise to the loss
of grip underneath as you skid.

You're learning the edge.
This crisp morning you walk old shoes
with the grace of a child skipping
in summer. The tips of your fingers
retain the touch of the skin
on the ears of your sons.
And even if it rains, just let it rain:
still you will sprinkle your lawn
tonight in the dark.

II.

On Course

The first two tacks were a wide zig-zag
that set me deep in this gray and abstract
compass-point where the wind is coming from.
West-by-southwest. I'm so far out from where
the sandbar trips the water into my dark Third Coast

that I can't make out in the rumple of dunes behind me
Three Surfers' Peak, that landmark for Lost Valley —
the one name we've ever found for home. The first tack
took me south; the second stretched longer west.
Before the final third of the journey I pause, point up the wind,

let the sails luff. The old contention is done.
I need some Michigan treeline in my eye. I turn.
The sail snaps full and jerks the little boat,
the prow swings to and starts to dive and run.
I re-rig the tackle light

because now I own the wind I have put behind me,
go where it blows, and it blows a straight course
to a touchable distance northeast, to fire
and some supper, let's say, red splotch of cottage
on the thin string of beach. I bind to the cleat

the tugging lines, then float my hands adrift;
as if in sleep I lift the daggerboard out
and let myself plane like a sudden surfer
exploding out of the gray into blue and white.
So this is the run that being lost was for.

Married to nothing but weather, I lean back
with the waking tiller and try to map out
the old high ways of stars I will not need
that fall unseen through the afternoon blaze of sky.
When I touch the breakers ahead,
the wind will pass me along from the surge

of one whitecap to the splash
of the next, the next, the next.
I ride that easy heartbeat all the way home.

Junior High

We skate out onto thin ice after nine,
but we're safe. There's concrete
tennis court beneath and floodlights above.
The little kids on wobbly ankles, pushing
their mothers' kitchen chairs, have gone;
the easy high-school crowd is laughing into cars.
Fewer now and alone, we dare to skate
boys with girls. The snow holds its breath.

Through woolen mittens and coats
we feel each other's backs, alive.
We shout and laugh to the dark
while beyond our yellow square of light
the houses of the town going small and orange
are ticking and ticking their clocks.

Lake Michigan Sand Cherries

Good children know that anything bitter
is wrong — so we knew the squat
dark plants on the beach were poison.
But within those rims of white sand-blows
the fruits shone so olive-blackly,
low in the wind, that I once broke through

with my right incisor tooth and my sister
said I would die but I didn't
even get sick or struck from behind
by God or lightning the way you would
if you were at a roadhouse dance
downshore at Saugatuck, say
(that's on the way to Chicago) —

so I forgot about them. They had lost
their Dutch theological sting.
We might as well have called them beach plums
the way I hear the rich resorters do
at Cape Cod. We called them nothing at all.

But there's a whirl of a woman comes down
from a hundred miles upshore
where the wind keeps you loving the earth,
and she drops them like notes in a yellow scarf
with an ease I could almost sing about.
I look at this dark-ruby red she has picked

and preserved and sent me in glass,
labeled *sand cherry / 8-82.* I taste
its dangerous lilt toward a dance
for the month of my birth, the wild tang
the Indians call Black Cherry Moon,
and I pray that all her moves
may continue to wink such graces.

Skating It Off

On blustery days, iced in,
I lash up the biting thongs
of ancestral wooden skates.
I lean into cheering winds
down old Frisian canals,
hands behind my back,
determined to show her.
But I have no cap or scarf
to brighten the streaming air,
I always shiver and swerve
and almost blow off the margin
and then the thin page cracks
and I splash through.

This time I'm going
to win the silver skates.
Watch: red tile roofs
under which we won't live
sail past while the bare arms
of only windmills wave
and I glide like butter
from stroke to long stroke,
leaving alternate wakes
of Delft-blue sparks
smoking high in the elms
behind, all the way into
the lights of Dokkum

before I notice that no one
is watching, she is not there.

Ways to Measure

Weigh raindrops in the fall
and you can feel
the speed at which the cold is coming in.

The absence of the son who died
grows tall in the doorway
where he had them mark his eighteen years
inch by inch.

A measure for decorum:
as restrained as the lunatic cabbage,
which opens only to moonlight.

Her anger one night was two cups
of gin. He got the moon
down to just the size of his fist.

A student said about a poem by Hardy,
"I wonder why he called it a lonely house.
There seems to be
at least one other person living there."

Ghazal: Some Aches Are Good

Each winter I mislay the summer, but last Christmas day
beach sand shone bright through the dark of a drawer.

Up close a star is not points, it's a stone in a stream,
light circling like the memory of a hat.

The whores back home worked on Commerce Street and their sheets
were gathered in and washed by the Sunshine Laundry.

Some aches are good: green plums, lifting a scab on a knee,
stretching a sprained ankle far down the bed in the morning.

I almost remember hunching in dark at a shore
before my father came with a light to find me.

Waving

When they propped my Grandma high up
in the oxygen tent, she started
to bob just slightly up and down, up
and down. She nodded and smiled
through the plastic window,
then blushing in white she waved
from the sleek little one-horse cutter
her dapper young Frisian-
American husband just bought, waved
to us through blue-tint isinglass
as she clipped down the immigrant streets
of southside Chicago sixty years before
her astonished grandson stood there,
coached by an uncle, and waved good-bye.

Reconciliation

The punishment was always just
to be alone. Its only sentence
was voices through window and floor,
light holding on
till talk ran down with the sky
toward darkness and sleep.

For the life of us
we didn't use words at our house.
Sadness was a shut door, love
was clean smells, the porch light.
So forgiveness even now
is a trip through night going cool,

engine fumes droning underfoot,
horns, night people I hear
and never see, gravity leaning me right
and then left over sudden pools of streetlight.
It is crunch and ping of gravel under tires,
a farm barking soft and clear, me

drowsing in the night's skin.
I don't want to break it, I only stir soft
against my father's white shirt blurred green
by dashlights to feel his daydream
of lifting a son from damp sheets,
the tight arms of two making both of us

one and half-asleep down steps
and over the grass. Waves nudge our shoreline
awake, but I only come back,
eyes full of light, at the ice cream store:
mica, ice cream, white shirt, star.

Interlude: Translations

Translation is a kind of transubstantiation; one poem becomes another. . . . The poem moves from life to language, the translation moves from language to life; both . . . try to identify the invisible, what's between the lines, the mysterious implications.

Anne Michaels

I. Fifteen Poems from Friesland

Experiments

For Willem de Jong

And after feeling the joy of shaping the world
God saw the forlorn stretches of desert
And so He sent to poets the fantasies
That steal along under the wordless space.
Now watch the leopards and antelopes stumble
Out of the tropics into the light, bewitched,
Crossing the heated jungles of the mind
To drink beside the heart, and at its streams.

Sjoerd Spanninga (1906-1985)

Stanzas for My Son

Don't curse with your mouth
if you suddenly come on an owl
lamenting above the overgrown yard
of Europe's nighttime rubble.

If you have to sometimes dip your bread
in tears, still stand faithful watch
through the night over this old land:
grieve at our grave, but not without hope.

Keep silence often and share your blanket
with those who can take the world's sorrow —
but don't dress yourself in scarlet clothes,
in the glaring costume of the fool.

Don't get caught up in every crowd
that scowls or looks askance at the spoils
the good earth gives. And if they hoist
stormflags on Tiber or Seine or Thames,

tighten the black crepe to muffle your drum.
Don't march along with the swelling music.
Son, follow no other way than this:
accept being a stranger.

Douwe A. Tamminga (1909-2002)

Two Miniatures

Windmill

The sail-arms turn and turn without making sense,
totally blind to any reason or gain
in their vain and clean trajectory through space.
But inside, huge stones roll and scour,
the wooden cogwheels wrestle in the dark
and grind rough fields of grain into tenuous flour.

Prayer

Lord, let me be like some grubby field bird
who doesn't establish a kingdom in the trees,
but somehow still gets along in your storms
and always comes out to dry again in your sun,
and time after time, as an upstart from the brush,
darts and dives the furrows: a startle of sparrow.

Douwe A. Tamminga

Images of a Summer Evening

Smell of hay across the wide, smooth water,
  White poplars rustling along the far side
  Of the farmyard where ducks now nap, tired
From all their wet up-ending and chatter.

It's getting late; the western red dies down
  And the blue carpet with golden stars
  Bends over all: birds, cattle, and flowers
Now sleep — sky hushes every song and sound.

A fine tsjalk* floats past, its black sails flap;
  An eddy dances along and breaks the reflection
  Of farmhouse and trees shaped in the shining wet.

The picture trembles but finally comes to lie
  Still, while ripples glide ashore — and mild
  And full the barge-woman's song floats by.

J.B. Schepers (1865-1937)

*tsjalk: a high-masted Frisian cargo barge

Midsummer

Midsummer. Cruel and howling-sharp the sickles
cut through the stalks which droop with grains;
one full slash, one broad and flashing sweep
through the thick, and the grass is beaten down.

Even so, sunrays draw out of that dying life
of green and flowers — cut down in full growth
while they strained for the shine of the sky —
the deep dark blossom of heavy fragrances.

Tomorrow, singed dry by the sun,
it will be shaken crisp and loose by the rakes,
the wagons stacked high and higher, rocking-full
wagonloads filling the threshing floor and the sheds.

Then, at night, when a soft breeze shivers through
and a bird cries sad in the half-light,
cool dew rinses the smarting wounds
and life shoots fresh from the broken sod.

In the field where a green pulse down in its scars
is dreaming of ripeness and the rustle in winds,
warm lips bite themselves down to the blood,
young eyes stare themselves blind in the dark.

Plump grainheads heavy with shining fruits will fall
before the sickle in sun and warm air;
fierce youth springs up to avenge what has died
and forever this flashing keeps its awful balance.

Jelle H. Brower (1900-1981)

Song of Songs

may the third 19seventytwo
a gentle swirling of grass-smell
drives through my green-bleeding blood
wind and sea strutting through my senses

in light that's hard to hold
I can take or leave the landscape
while trees jauntily
break the distances

therefore I retreat
among the little larks
and brush the strings
from space that I
play into sound
in my closet of silence
sounds which the tides&time at long last
let go

Tsjêbbe Hettinga (b. 1949)

From In the Enchantment of the Depth between Light and Light

Stanza 3

evening like a cool tired waiter lays the beer-cloth
over the muffled city secretly closing doors
against the mobs created in the darkest shades
while the moon that anarchist among the lampposts
laces from the leafy light an unsteady garland for death
and now like a wayward child straggling far behind
and pulling crazy faces in the gambling dens and
    halls-of-mirrors
of our time-bound egos we march through thin spaces
of our echoes across warm tiles to a drab room
where smoke moves like the mist off ditches
under the lamps which spread evenly over
    the table stark contrasts
of light, as in Van Gogh's painting, spread
    over an evening meal,
and here too wrinkled faces trying to hide sorrow.

Tsjêbbe Hettinga

The Kite

I am the thought-made-paper
the design transmitted from father to son
the frame fleshed tight
held fast with bone-glue
my face in the image of man
my tail in the image of beast

the tight line feels good on the ribs
(drunkenness is not becoming to kites)
I rise lovely from a hand
and stand steep over the city
there is not enough cord for high festival
my friend is fooling with old newspapers

telegraphed words huddle near me up here
ashamed I shake my head no
I hum silent praise to loose string
and fall down again on my shadow

I am crucified head-down and
my corpse makes static on the phone

Geart Van Der Zwaag (1924-1989)

The Sterile Ones

they never walk the range of a poem
on its trip from sounds to thoughts
they have forbidden the tensions of rhythm
encamped behind the lines
of their own metered existence

a flicker of poetic image comes along
and they grasp armor and heave up shields
they only rhyme God's existence to thoughts about Him
too thick-skinned to go into the difference

Daniël Daen (b. 1942)

Lunch Break

from twelve to one
spread it with a fork, eat
gray peas and side-pork
and the Gospel According to Matthew
needs to be droned for half an hour
nap a little, wake with sour guts
that takes a quarter-hour
lay patriarchal doom on everyone
and yammer away at our mom
for the high price she pays the butcher for meat
there's the other quarter-hour
back to the fields to spread the shit

Daniël Daen

Wrappings

in the market
a man was walking
three sheets to the wind
holding in his hand
greasy newspaper

the eel that he
meant to take home
for his wife to make amends
for the drunk he was on
had slipped away

Jan J. Bylsma (b. 1932)

God, I'm Tired

God, I'm tired, I drag,
Is there nowhere a woman
Nowhere a crisp white bed,
Nothing known, no rock-hard faith
No somber noble feeling
Among the living souls?

Each day turns into its night.
Pain comes back — alone.
O cutting lightstar
Where are the other stars
That can flicker like the glints
From darkling eyes?

I think of the shadows that lower
Black brows over deep eyes
And the sighs, the steady breathing,
And the smiles, and the ship
Of dreams that sails
The nightwind through the night.

G.N. Visser (1910-2001)

From **First and Last**

5

If I had been a tree
I would have stood
In one of those little churchyards
Hedged in by a circle of privet.
There they come, Sunday afternoons,
To read the gravestones
To brush aside a few wild grasses
Or scratch the moss off a name:
I would like to murmur something
Low beneath what they know they hear,
And one who stayed the last,
Lonely and still on her bench,
I would gently shadow.

Theun De Vries (1907-2005)

Autumn House

the rooms with music
are closed the copper path
has strangled shut
autumn is lying
on windowsills

the garden slowly
takes off its clothes
how red just then
was her skirt
at the windows
the nightfrost waits
the pond gets covered

stone-cold stairway
without a runner
looking glass which doesn't
hang there

the back door sleeps
in its hinges
autumn drags itself
through spidersilk
and slowly
the gutter drips

Tsjitte Piebenga (1935-2007)

Sailing-Barges at Night

It has passed;
the cold light gone, a dim light left, blind
from one bank to the other over the water,
a knocking and asking delicately
against the black barges, until
it just disappeared.

Boats at night.
It was a dark land and a black sky,
little lights in the small waves, else nothing
except for the sound of a child, a hush:
the intimate breath of the canal.

Where is it blown
as the reeds rustle on stalks turning brown
and sigh on the dreary banks?
We slide our last boat ashore
and doze off — the currents
have drifted farther.

J.D. De Jong (1912-1996)

II. Seven Poems from Present-Day Israel

Translated by Moshe Dor and Rod Jellema

Summer

Summer calls for thorn fires;
up the unmentionable heavens,
the sun, roll-
ing itself over, turns away.

The scorched fields all around wave
here and there green slashes of grain,
wounds not yet scarred over. The grave truth
cannot be hidden by heat from
the tongue stuck out by
dumbstruck heaven, so unspeakably

dead: we can't disprove these scores and scores
of dead who multiply every day;
we watch with eyes that are also — how else
can we say it? — undeniably dead.
The widows after all
are young. The mothers
are hard of hearing. We turn

our faces aside, but truth is there, the war,
so surely devouring, summer after summer,
in this death-deranged and blood-dreaming land.

Tuvia Ruebner (b. 1929)

And the Mother's Face in the Scales

And if this time it's oh well the neighbors' son
who's left nothing to earth
and if this time it's the neighbors'
son and the wind didn't stand still and the tree
wasn't uprooted and the dog barked

we said terrible, terrible it's
terrible. Thank God, the neighbors' son
God be praised, the neighbors'
son —
has it not dragged on for years, years for
each moment that we sharply listened for
the voice from beyond the line saying I'm fine, O.K., whole,

until everything unforgiven is decreed and sealed?
And his parents are old
and that's the end. And how to look — they're fossilized
people — how look in the dumbfounded faces being weighed,
the face of a dying animal the father's face
and the mother's face
who's no longer a mother and is faceless in the scales?

Tuvia Ruebner

She Was in Jerusalem

1

She was in Jerusalem,
agreed to visit the Wailing Wall
boasting, *I'm not religious.*

In the note that she didn't press
among the prayers that others press
between stones, into the cracks in the wall,

she wrote many things
about me, her, about Jerusalem.

2

I too was in Jerusalem,
went to the Wailing Wall.
I'm not religious.
In all the notes that became my poems
my only prayer
has been that I may hold onto
the dignity and the image
of being human
and hold the loves of my heart.

3

I have no Wall in Jerusalem.
I have no mosque in Jerusalem.
I have no church in Jerusalem.

My Jerusalem
is most beautiful among women.
She is the sad tune,
and the note and the poem
on which is written,

Jerusalem,
I'll come back, soon.

Na'im Araidi (b. 1950)

Looking toward Jerusalem

Maybe we should gather
all the boulders
in the hills of Jerusalem.
Maybe we should build another Wall
another mosque
another church.
Maybe

we should bury all past wrongs,
maybe
we should build at last
another city, but not
in the hills of Jerusalem.

We shall call it Jerusalem.

Na'im Araidi

The Coastal Road, before Dawn

It's still non-light, the very hesitation,
the pause between dark and the hazy glow
through which the angel saw only dimly
the pale lintels of those doomed to receive
his visitation of death. From the distant darkness,
nearer and nearer, rolling like thunder,
the roar of heavy trucks. They are weighted down
with unimaginable horror, as if arriving from
the depths of a new Dante's Inferno —
     And then the birds

Moshe Dor (b. 1932)

Spring

A mild sun deciphers
The ancient parchment of my skin
in this new land, young and brazen.

The waters of the seas keep warming,
they rise and rise as if they could drown
the rainbow's deep-held promise.

But if, in some wet abyss, a new
history is forming, spawning mollusks
and eels too huge to imagine,
it is sure to burst out of the deep
With an insatiable passion for light.

This will happen when I am gone
beyond the forgetting of a memory.
But just now, as you draw near,
hurry on your way, don't stand
between me and the sun.

Moshe Dor

Guesses

All day the crows cried out their caws of anguish
falling silent only after dusk. We didn't know

why they shrieked and why they fell silent. Standing
on the path by the mown grass we wondered:

was it an outcry against the random shedding of blood
or their dismay over the rotting of society's moorings?

We tried to guess if it stopped at dusk because nobody cared
or because even the caring ones have given up.

Then the moon, stained red, climbed up over the hills,
round and shiny like the platter that carried

the severed head of John — and in sudden dread,
tongue-lost, we rushed to our houses and locked the doors behind us.

Moshe Dor

From *A Slender Grace* (2004)

Words Take Water's Way

The wash of waves is scouring
and sanding words down to stones
to shine what they show.
Stranded consonants, dry chunks,
crave the liquidity of vowels.
Words take water's way.
It's like a sleep, the slip
through half light while the stars
scatter and move beyond us.
Softer than the air that wakes us,
sleep is water of no weight at all,
loosening us adrift in swirls
of currents, where charts are useless.

When Adam, drowsy, felt
his uncharted ways into speech,
drifting the flow of vowels,
his heart must have leaped like his tongue
from one surprise to the next,
rocks and boulders like sculpted
talismans jutting out, roiling the narrow
river that Yahweh had left him.
And Adam's mouth, holding
the feel of whirl, of crack,
of round, float, and salt,

formed for itself sonorities
of *ripple, edge, horse,*
of *crunch,* and *moon,*
shaping out of the stream of words
his praise and wonder,
the pictures in his head, sounds
that would speak his loneliness,
a few lines that might stay.
He freed us, all of us
Adam's children, free in play
to pocket words like stones
found on the shores, to arrange them

in settings only dreamed,
as many settings
as there are stars in the sky.

The Housekite

The politicians sometimes talk as though [Washington's]
troubled streets are only an obstacle between their offices
and their homes, as though their homes are luxurious houseboats
independently afloat somewhere on the crystal seas.

The Washington Post

There's this poet invited me onto his housekite,
thin walls free in endless blue sky, the old lure
of matter transfigured as pure light and air.
But I worry that he'll pay out too much line
and he and his housekite won't make it back.

I imagine the thrill of drifting through clouds with him
and spinning some lazy loops while holding
onto his kitchen table — but I know I'd be
hunched there, working designs for string worms,
glue moths, a Brown-Headed Kitepecker, anything

to bring him low, lower than porch lights, down
into houses with windows that stick but look out
onto gobs of green too dark for flight,
houses heavy with ovens and history and shoes,
their possible moons suspended in two mugs of ale.

He's up there now on a test flight. Next time
his housekite could get so high it's only a vapor.
I'm sending a punched note up the tensing string
to wake him from his spirity dream of home.
It's down here, my note says. *Keep in touch.*

For Donald Petersen

Think Narrow

One of six million rods or cones
in the eye will flash one cell
of the billion in the brain
at the end of the thread of optic nerve
to catch a single ray from a streetlight
as it bounces off black water
asleep in a pothole.

This predicts the way the stem
of a coconut palm
leans long and far away
into pinpoints of light we call stars.
Come dawn, a split second of music
in the thin sing of a finch
will slip into the crack between two notes
the way a tiny lizard darted just now
into a slit in the terrace wall.

Think narrow. Think the line of light
that leapt under the bedroom door
to save the frightened child who was you.
Your thin escape from being someone else.
The slender grace of a sudden thought
that takes you past your self, walking

the good gray heavy town,
the bulge and muscle and long bone
that enables a wisp of thought to walk
these streets, themselves created by thought.
Think how we stride the wide earth
pressing down our weight and our love,
exulting in the plump swell of growth,
knowing the narrow gift of incarnality
is ours by the skin of our teeth.

Ice Age

circa 1932

The wet brown canvas
that covers the load of ice
smells like mushrooms sour
under blackening leaves
deep in a woods.
But with one heave the iceman
peels it back
and flings open his kingdom
to August daylight.

The shine of his pick
cracks ahead of its point
down seams of the ice blocks,
it splits open ravines and valleys
as he showers meteors skyward
in a spray of rainbow cold.

Some days he'd toss us crystal
shards as we watched from the curb.
With a *chuuunk* of the tongs
he'd heft a block of ice
high onto the blue of his shoulder
darkened to black by water.

It comes back, that ache
through the teeth while staring at ice,
waking up the dreamed geographies
between the spin of star-ice in space
and the warm tar paving of home —

a world, the shakes
of an idling truck, a stain
that spreads, two boys and a dog,
a rusted ice pick calling
far down in a drawer.

For Robert Burton

Bicycle Parts

(1) The Frame

Strip it of all its odd appendages,
its wheels and fenders, handlebars, saddle seat,
fork, its pedals and kickstand, and what
you come down to discover is a harp.

Mine was blue, just darker blue than sky
blue, and I knew somehow (the way
the deaf must know of something like music)
that mine was in touch with an angel.

Usually I flung it on the ground
wherever I jumped off, as all boys do,
but just a few times I must have seen
the real shape of the harp by itself,

because I remember now a sense
of narrow strings in sudden slants of light
that made me gentle it down into the grass
so maybe more than wind might find it there.

(2) Spokes

They leapt into sight under corner streetlights, singing
as bright a falsetto as candles in church Christmas Eve:
the spokes, cold rays, narrow fingers that shook
themselves off like a shower of needles, shooting
the outcasts of houselight and headlight back out to space.

Sometimes I try to shake off sleep by thinking
to wake again in that thunderstorm night
when a silver bike wheel turned, all by itself,
in flashes of lightning out back
in the vacant lot behind my childhood.

From my dark window that time I rubbed my eyes
and simply saw a fallen star, orbiting
out of our neighborhood ballfield's quackgrass,
turning, slowly untangling his wings. . . .

I watched spokes a lot after that
but never told about him till now, long after
any boy might ride a bike at night anymore
past the streetlight outside my apartment window.

(3) The Sprocket

It had to evolve slowly,
no one could have thought of this thing
all at once, this sprocket
lop-siding a sideways axis
winding gravity into itself and
concentrating a crotch
as a starting point,
then gnawing its way backward

with regular teeth down a dirty chain
to its smaller self on another axle,
propelling the whole engine ahead from behind.
With its legs bent into painful circles
and driven by the grinding of sprocket,
this rolling contraption (parsons far back
might have roared) came clanging right out of Hell.

Our feet harnessed to an arc
to pump up and down in alternate strokes
(instead of the off-balance/balance-slowly-
forward-motion that God intended legs for),
no one would have thought us able
to thrust this artifice bearing ourselves

forward swiftly far out for miles
and miles through wind with nothing, nothing
but this new momentum to keep us upright.

(4) Fenders

They get their name from fending off earth and mud,
but try to see how they do it: not like a Dutch housewife,
armed with brush and cleanser to attack the dirt,
but like a gardener who lifts the soil to smell it
and likes to return all things to their proper places.
They keep us from having to fend for ourselves.
They lay the mud and dust back down on the road
like hands that are healing or saying a blessing.
So maybe they *are* women after all, these fenders, skirted,
curved for grace, tough — these mysterious lovers.

(5) The Front Tire

The front tire
of the bike
throws itself down
in the street
like a prayer rug
so you can beg
mercy and peace,
then leaps
to fling itself
up the back
of the circle,
rising like bells
up the steep
just in time

to let go &
fling itself
down again,
good priest
keeping you
off the street
while slipping
up the back
collecting the beads

of holy water
it sprinkles
out in front
and then picks up
again, again
a perpetual
prayer.

(6) Bicycle Seats

The row of little monuments
in the schoolyard bike rack
these gentle hands, palms up

intimate but never shy
these nuzzlers

that hold like the sacristy
the mysterious vessels

each a little shrine
raised to await
the coming miracle.

Letter to Lewis Smedes about God's Presence

I have to look in cracks and crevices.
Don't tell me how God's mercy
is as wide as the ocean, as deep as the sea.
I already believe it, but that infinite prospect
gets farther away the more we mouth it.
I thank you for lamenting His absences —
from marriages going mad, from the deaths
of your son and mine, from the inescapable
terrors of history: Treblinka. Viet Nam.
September Eleven. It's hard to celebrate
His invisible Presence in the sacrament
while seeing His visible absence from the world.

This must be why mystics and poets record
the slender incursions of splintered light,
echoes, fragments, odd words and phrases
like flashes through darkened hallways.
These stabs remind me that the proud
and portly old church is really only
that cut green slip grafted into a tiny nick
that merciful God Himself slit into the stem
of His chosen Judah. The thin and tenuous
thread we hang by, so astonishing,
is the metaphor I need at the shoreline
of all those immeasurable oceans of love.

Adapted from an e-mail discussion, Summer 2002

The Pineapple Poem

A slash of blade: the precise geometry
of pineapple armor nicked with steel
releases a sweet, pale sting of vapor
that spins and dizzies the room.
Already in 1513, a Spanish chronicler
of New World wonders reported this strange
"fragrance of more-than-perfect peaches,
partaking somewhat of quinces." His praise,
the first in writing, hummed on for 3,000 words.

If he were writing now, Gonzalo Fernandez
would tell us to cut it fresh.
That little crunch of tart then spurt
of sweet under the tooth comes best
if you slice it long like strips of melon,
the way dusty farmers have always done
under hot Brazilian suns. Suck a narrow
slice, hold it long in the mouth.
It keeps its sharp but slowly honeys home
as the juice seeps under the tongue
down where taste buds wait for liquids.

Andrew Marvell, giving thanks for fruits
of Bermuda, was struck by the way this tiny
tree gives up its life to bear a single fruit.
He saw the New World waving at the Old
a holy symbol of the sacrificial Tree —
and so, before pineapples signaled the status
and wealth of glass greenhouses, before they sang
hospitality from doorways and the porcelain
dinnerware of mansions and inns, they bloomed
as finials gracing English churches.
The people could almost taste exotic charity.

We retain some ceremony. Look at the way
we remove its emerald crown, the way
we help it lay down its life in rings
buried in the glistening fat of a ham

we've criss-crossed, then nailed with cloves.
Its acid-sweet drizzle wakens the flesh,
till all traces of pigblood, dry wood, squeal,
rude smoke in the eyes are transfigured,
and the sanctified centerpiece sings its descant
to white linen and silver, to the crystalware
brimming with the royal red of wine.

And there's the pious way our mothers revived us
from two decades of depression and wars
by turning the world on Sundays upside-down:
they'd lay the yellow rings, sticky with sugared
hot butter, to anchor the cake to its floor,
certain that the living spirit would rise
in the oven clean through to the top,
which then became, with one flip, the bottom,
enthroning pineapple, making everything right. †

For Michael Olmert

Come Winter

Our two most beautiful words
said Henry James
are *summer* and *afternoon,*
and today he's almost right.

Out of the leaves of an oak
that hums like Schubert
a breeze shakes flocks
of sunlight abounding
across the lawn

while little beads
skate their frosty tracks
all over my glass of pilsner,
and now there's the distant
thwack of a screen door
and a blackbird's whistle
riding above the muffled shouts
of boys playing baseball
in a vacant lot
three blocks or sixty years away.

But such a day sits still.
Just another summer afternoon
that can't get past itself,
end of the line,
like the faded red boxcars
long years ago, left on a spur
in hot yellowing grass
in a wash of light
nowhere to go.

I pick up my beer and
turn back inside,
thinking there has to be more,
remembering in winter
lying still dark mornings
before the window drifted into place,

musing how snow rounds off
all edges of roofs and street signs,
how it curves and softens
a world in the same way that images,
dreams, imaginings
made and shaped the creation
as they rose out of holy *darkness*
that's *on the face of the deep.*

So "the dead of winter"
is an old deception, a lie,
undone by swelling twigs
and pregnant bears asleep,
by the oily smell of the
baseball glove in the closet.
Winter is a girl who skips
over patches of dirty slush
with bright barrettes in her hair.
Winter makes *(yes!)* spirit visible
in the very steam from our mouths.
Call it a certain hope,

it finally raises from the dark
that stranger hope of a second coming
of the One who hung out the stars
at the world's beginning, coming
not to scourge and burn
and blow up the world
and nail it to our failings
but to embrace and infuse it,
lighting up our recall
of Eden and who we are,
bringing us back to where
we can make the world right,

knowing again that
summer and *afternoon*
live and endure
only out of the
working depths of
winter and *morning.*

Beneath the Signals of the Car Pool Radio, 1999

Five days a week the car pool radio
keeps us from noticing how I-270
runs away like we might have done in our youth
from suburban streets called home,
past broken fences and silos, open fields,
to our labs. It drowns out the budgets
which almost assure us that the science we do
can now create every decade or so
a new and almost perfectly adequate god.

We don't admit we can't build even a worm,
and nobody asks. There's never much talk
above the radio — sometimes a word
on the Redskins or where we're from.
They win or lose. No one is from here.

This late afternoon, aimed back at Bethesda,
I'm thinking how the radio search-buttons work,
how it's a thin line of absence of static
that locks in the dial. I wonder
if a similar absence, a *nothing*,
might fine-tune the rest of our lives —

what is it that signals, for example,
the drinks we'll mix tonight for our wives?
It's late March — we're locked into daiquiris.
And when the blenders hum over hedges
across our lawns, I'm almost afraid
I'll hear again the echo of Ohio snowplows
sighing from far, and then a wind
and the scraping of skate blades on ice.

Surely such longings reveal some residual good.
Yet how can minds like ours — a mind like mine,
slicing DNA to near infinity —
weep, or want to kick the family cat?
What signals miss us when we turn the music loud?

Suspended between the spin of nuclei
and the evening news, expecting distortions,
I try to think just how it can be
that we sometimes find ourselves under trees
in each other's fenced back yards,
at each other's charcoal fires —

how we eat together the sacrificial meat,
and stare. The smoke can unroll
like holy scrolls, like an unread past
we're losing. Right now, streaking
out of shadows as we pass a shopping mall,
I try to think: What if the past, like our science,
is a meaning that hasn't finished?

The question dies beneath some car pool banter
I feel obliged to enter. Small talk
of women. I grunt assent to a slur
more cruel than funny while stale radio lyrics
of unrequited love whine over jangled strings.
The singer's swagger ignores, as I do,
what we almost know: that it's an insult
to a woman to be loved by an unhappy man.

We don't talk much about it, how our women,
weary of propping our weaknesses up
against our statistical heart attacks,
are letting us go. They will not be anymore
like curved little boats in their slips that tilt
and sway the stylish names we give them
for all the club to admire.

The music thumps louder. I want to shout,
Turn the radio down, we never meant
this old song, this lie that men are strong.
It's older than fear of fire,
deeper than war cries, this hatred we have
of the wide and cold dark spaces behind the dials
that send out only interference.
There's something we lost that we fear
to listen for in the static.

But I've already shut the door, waved
the car pool off, I'm walking mute
up my driveway, closer every night
to the century's end, locked on the beam
of yellow from the little porch light.

A Wedding Toast

In seven meanings of the word, may this couple be *flush:*

because they are

(1) a sudden fresh and abundant growth,
a glow of light or color; vigor, rushing flow;
a blending of *flash* and *blush;*

and because they now become

(2) in direct contact, contiguous surfaces,
forming one plane — or
(3) a meld of one suit (such as hearts),

may all their days together be

(4) prosperous, (5) lusty, (6) full to overflowing,
(7) as a sudden rising of birds.

Reach

. . . a man's reach should exceed his grasp,
or what's a heaven for?
Robert Browning

This wish to touch the silky down
along the downward swooning
curve of a swan's neck:
look how it pulses and twists away
into the swelling mound of muscle

at the base of his wings, those sails
that can thunder white
into the darkest or bluest skies.

There must be fiery quivers
tensing tight beneath the folds
of quiet feathers,

nerve lines set to trill like mine
as my hand inches close to feel
this snowstorm warmly drifting.

But he doesn't flinch. Calmly
his orange-webbed engines
ignite and push soft ripples
into a wake as he moves off
downstream, free to ignore me.

The Replay

The third day after Epiphany Sunday, 1996

That shine of green patch in the sky I saw
waving a sign through fog and wet branches —
three dawns have passed, and still I wonder
what I saw.

Maybe the paper from a gift box of pears, green tissue
the wind took up with, lifting the skirt sky high,
over the rooftop at the end of my street, the little
nunnery

where the sisters who teach at Our Lady of Lourdes,
freed from black habits, shine their Monday windows.
But it also might be what their breaths told winter
in morning prayer,

thanking God for glass, lessons, fresh streams
of light. Surely it wasn't what first I thought —
a green kite rudely jerked from a child's hand. This thing
held steady

its diamond shape as it rose, this image
that would prompt any nun who might look up
to cross herself. But now that it's blown far past
Our Lady, it is

oriental green brocade ripped from the cloak
of an ancient king, interweaving a swatch of song
from a waitress — African, walking alone to an early bus,
her prayer snagged

and riding a star — and now it arcs through the doze
of an old night watchman, tending his brickyard, watching
from seven towns west of here, who shrugs off his whim to
follow the star —

not meant for the likes of him, he says, too much
like a dream. He needs some coffee. And anyway it's almost
morning, he says, almost light now, almost time to go home and
sleep it off.

Secondary Ed.

In high school no teacher told us
that algebra's abstract equations
glue together a near-infinity
of molecules and tractors and stars,
or that geometry lays out
the shape and essence
of the mind's argument with itself.
No one said how the cadences
and leaps of the human heart
imprint themselves on an underlay
the Greeks measured and called iambic.

Failing to stay the set courses,
I listened out of school
to nickel junk-shop recordings
by the Hot Five Jelly Roll & Bix,
found the scale of things,
how separate arcs relate, heard
some counterpoint, caught a sense
of lines that crystallize into shapes
formed by the pressures inside them.

Such wild hot math helped me
sneak into college without a diploma
and cut me wide open to Plato &
Shakespeare, then Homer, Keats.
Still — why does stirred water
form bubbles that are perfect spheres?
And how does anyone understand
the mysterious presence of *pi?*

For Jack Kuipers

We Used to Grade God's Sunsets
from the Lost Valley Beach

Why we really watched we never said.
The play of spectral light, but maybe also
the coming dark, and the need to trust
that the fire dying down before us
into Lake Michigan's cold waves
would rise again behind us.
Our arch and witty critiques
covered our failures to say what we saw.

The madcap mockery of grading God as though
He were a struggling student artist
(*Cut loose, strip it down, study Matisse*
and risk something, something unseen —
C-plus, keep trying — that sort of thing)
only hid our fear of His weather
howling through the galaxies. We humored
a terrible truth: that nature gives us hope
only in flashes, split seconds, one
at a time, fired in a blaze of beauty.

Picking apart those merely actual sunsets,
we stumbled into knowing the artist's job:
to sort out, then to seize and work an insight
until it's transformed into permanence.
And God, brushing in for us the business
of clouds and sky, really is a hawker
of clichés, a sentimental hack as a painter.
He means to be. He leaves it to us
to catch and revise, to find the forms
of how and who in this world we really are
and would be, to see how much promise there is
on a hurtling planet, swung from a thread
of light and saved by nothing but grace. †

Green Beans

The bean is a graceful, confiding, engaging vine;
but you never can put beans into poetry. . . .
There is no dignity in the bean.

Charles Dudley Warner

(1)
Spring-loaded vines
on tendrils
shinny up skinny
poles and
shoot for the sun.
Their leavings are
heart shapes that
pinch to life
small yellow curves
that plump
like the knuckles
on babies' hands.
Each nub
lengthens down
to a green
velvet composure
that will curtsy
and sway in the wind.

(2)
No need to slit the tight skin
down to its pearls. Just snap

the stem and bite. The coldest
spring water never rinses away

the holy scent of turned earth
slendered into a bean, that trace

it holds of wild green smoke.
Relaxed in steam and slathered

in buttery gold, each one of
these peasants, when summoned

to the royal red silk
banquet hall of your mouth,

will loyally serve its fare,
presenting with quiet dignity

small mists of sweetgrass, pineroot,
peat, seawater, ancient stone.

New Era, Michigan

Founded 1887 Pop. 461
Our seven churches welcome you

A few Saturday women in their habits of denim
early cross the aisles of our only supermarket.
Behind the walls of awakened houses, others
push and pull the wheezing lungs of vacuums,
blending a choir of voices that hymn the town
to rid itself of the dust of one more week.
Breakfast waits for children quietly bowed
before the flickering colored lights on screens;
they make no sign of disbelief or belief
in the flying and falling figures who squeal
and boom in voices from other worlds.
Men of the town, with two days off,
take communion of muffled laughs and grunts
under the hoods of each other's idling pickups,
while the glacial old lake, beyond the dunes,
falls to its knees and lays its hands on our shore,
up and down, and now the teens rise from their beds
to begin their seventh-day pilgrimage
toward the inland shopping mall three towns away.

Snow Emergency Route

Maryland suburbs,
Washington, D.C.

History spins its wheels down our avenue.
While plumes of steam like doves fly from our mouths,
we shovel and push our way out, hail-fellow
strangers, pooling our muscles and wits
before the plow or the tow truck comes.
This whiteness could almost stick us together,

but we strain to break free. Each of us will either
drive a capsule of steel down city roads, or slide
underneath in lighted tubes, reading the *Post*.
Back to normal. Alone in office cubicles,
tapping the keystrokes that hope to unite a nation,
each of us can again keep a proper distance.

Young Man at the Laundromat Watching the Spinning Dryers

That blown scarf is bird-flocks
that weave through the wind and split the seams of light.
Tatted blue-jay swatches fly with parrot greens
and dartings of yellow finch. A swish and they scatter,
haunted off by a bedsheet that drifts like snow,
then lifts up into dark when everything stumble-dries
forward again, flying head-over-dells and hill-
over-bells, flying almost out of the loom.
This young woman, reading *Glamour*, likes candlelight suppers.
I read her life by glances. Her placemats say felicity,
say grace. At the flight of a red bra I look down at my shoes.

Or else at dryer 4. It is pummeling
serious work-clothes black and blue.
This man is order and edge, homespun as the name
hammered onto the pockets. *Duke.* Nothing
here can shimmer, even the towels are beige
as mortar. I look for a leap of frivolous zags
or zigs on a shirt, for light green as slight as a child
or a wisp or whistle of pink. There ought to be
at least a lettered T-shirt reminder to him
of a crazy Chicago weekend with too much beer.
The only relief is the red shout of a hunter's sleeve.

I am folding. 6 and 4 are long gone home. Outside
the streetlights diminish the beating stars.
Only dryer 3 holds me in, and she is away.
I imagine her off at the market filling a basket
with fruit, everything round. I color her
ripe olive black, then hack a steamy, twisting path
through waving lemongrass. I ease my basket down
to the river, down to the river, find her there
in sunlight, out on the rocks, and now we two are silent
villagers waving a far hello along the river,
each of us pounding, pounding our underclothes on rocks.

Singing in the Shower

The throaty "caww" is familiar, but a musical warble
is produced only when [crows] think themselves unobserved.

The Columbia Encyclopedia,
2nd Edition

It's just natural. Even a crow
will sneak away from the flock
and all the racket of the rookery
to make a song, just for himself,
when nothing's there to hear him.

Sometimes I hear myself
as a *basso profundo* warbler:
it's the resonance you get
from four walls closing in,
even in on defeat. Just sing it out.

How pure the voices must have rung,
those monks at the St. Bernard Pass,
if not to God's ears to their own,
each praying hourly in his little stall
for travelers up near the snow line.

I risk a squeak and a caww now
and then, soaping up past loneliness,
singing out to my love *dum dee ho*
right through the lusty flats,
thinking myself unobserved.

Little Rock Barbeque

Old habits: taking my raincoat regardless of sky,
or the way I obfuscate with black *becauses* your fascination
with the colors of *nows*. I wonder how you can stand it.
Being trapped with me in some town like Little Rock,
for example, waiting an hour for a taxi to nowhere
special while my chattering drowns out all the spices
of last night's barbeque by debating with myself
if that word is African. And you, with a lilt of the only grace
that saves us, wonder aloud if I might like
to pursue that question sometime when I'm alone.
I go silent, and you flush out a surprise of startled birds
that our serious books insist on calling laughter.

Though I've now looked up in a serious book
the etymology of *barbeque*, I'll resist telling you
next Monday what it is because, alone again,
I'm going to phone to say, I would like to have you along
for rainstorms, restaurants, late taxis, the walks
along the longest avenues, wherever they take us.

For Michele

The Color of His Hunger

For the older addicts who sleep
and beg in these narrow streets
of Old San Juan, the color
of hunger is brown of stew
dissolving to gray. For the young

Harry, whose heroin still
can shoot his brain with rainbows
of sparks, hunger comes
blue, willowware blue, blue
of flame under his mother's kitchen

kettle in Duluth. Tonight it's the glow
through palm trees of the blue-
plate special fading into its poster
in the window of Café Tio Miguel
across the dark of Plaza San José.

But lately, as he stirs in the art shop doorway
near the cathedral, with its stained-glass
Madonna (bluer than the sky is far),
waves of hunger surf in to his waking,
and he has to shake off a sicker blue,

the puffed blue lips of the corpse
washed up last month on La Perla shore.
And maybe now he wakes to fear
a still worse blue, the cool
blue eyes that always gaze

past him into nothing at all,
never meeting his, the blue
unfocused vacancy I saw
mirrored this morning while I shaved
as I absently thought about Harry.

Some of the "Whats" That Are in a Name

My novelist friend, who thought our lunch
was booked for the Pleasant *Pheasant*,
drove northward into a flutter of bronze
that flushed up teal and red
from the hedges of her mind.
She rustled up a toss of greens
and a thin-stemmed *Pouilly-Fuissé*,
smoked trout and truffles
under crystal, frost on cut glass,
jewels splitting the candlelight,

while I, rattling south on the subway
to the Pleasant *Peasant*, lurched
the muddy road through furze and gorse
to a smoky hearth that reeked of
torn-up leeks afloat in turnip soup.
Wind in the rafters wafted a rich stink
of goat cheese and tallow that hung
over a slab table set for two with
the swill of royal brown mutton stew
in oaken bowls, and tankards of sack.

All through that memorable lunch at the *Pleasant*
Whatever, good talk soared and lumbered on
and flashed, all hammer knocks and startled wings,
while the food, whatever it was, got cold.

Aphrodite at Paphos, 1994

When I saw her gliding
naked through the surf
divine body of
perfect glistening flesh
I snapped up my
binoculars and they
blinded me normal again.

Take a Chance

If you cancel the trip to Innisfree
because it's raining, you may miss the quick
red rage of a torn leaf
before it gentles itself onto the quiet pool.

The tests warned him that his exceptional mind
was weakest for doing math, so math
is what he took up with holy awe,
forcing his dazzled way to insight.

If you always leave a nightlight burning
because as a child you got fearfully lost,
turn it off. The lights far out in the dark
are sending lifelines you never imagined.

The New Age seers, tracking the fates, may tell you
no — but take a chance. Just maybe that old
unbelievable Yahweh really did imprint you
with enough God Image to make you free to leap.

Still Life Waiting for Something to Start Again

There's a tight red bowl on the sill
near a rocking chair that's newly painted blue.
Nothing moves, not even a mind,
and if perhaps a spider behind the wall,
so still you'd hear it. The step
on the stair is the wind, only the wind.

When he scoured the sink to white,
hours ago, water rang against rust
in the pipes like a finger rubbing
the rim of a crystal glass.
He won't ask her where she's been,
the years. He made the idea of goblet
spill out on the table the idea of water,
but that was hours ago. There's still a trace.

An emptiness her size and shape
would move now to the window if he were God.
The centerpiece basket holds the woven
shape of the light from the open window
against the dark that starts to struggle
up from the street. She can see the long-gone
tram-track where it crossed itself
on its knees under gaslights, before their time.

The room holds its breath, its little tongues,
the bowl holds air like the open
throat of a bird just before it cries out.
That click and then that click
is the weather checking the steampipes
and it's a long time since he turned a page.
He has dusted everything, hours ago, he has
set the table for two, and now, now it is time

Bix Beiderbecke Composing Light, 1927-1931

Musical genius who could hardly read music,
jazz cornet player exiled by shame
from the classic Victorian house in Davenport,
he taught himself when he could at pianos
in lonely rooms and never said what he had caught:
sounds for the changes in light through five mutations.
In a Mist the first piece was called,
then *Candlelights* and *Cloudy,* then finally,
as a friend put them on paper, *Flashes* and *In the Dark.*

The notes are the sound of an aura
or the sound of pale yellow
as it plays off the corner of the eye
and darts away just when a child
will quickly turn the head to catch it.
As he feels for keys, the chords shiver
thin, a *mist* of light from Eden,
a primal catch in the breath.

Maybe it startled up the first time this kid
saw lights in the distance at night,
empty factories, houses lit low and lonely
down river from Davenport's docks,
or maybe the sparks from boats in fog
that cried their horns all over black water.

It might have been flutters one starless night
in the big dining room window, which were maybe
reflections of the *candle lights* — or were they
holy tongues of flame down a twisting road
that he looked for years later, outside,
taking Vera for a drive in his father's
1920 Davis 8? The road wasn't there.

Ivory keys in hollow rooms. If only
his fingers could align the ear of the mind
he'd see the sounds to take. To him it's spaces,
he dares to explore the spaces in his head.

Though some days they're only *cloudy*,
his fingers have to find those phrases
the spaces mean, touching them alive,
chords that don't yet exist.

Too late to learn like Ravel, studying structure
from paper. Twenty-eight and dying of booze.
Through eight years of hot cornet on bandstands
and jamming, he caught his music in *flashes*,
blew instant recompositions of themes
bent through silver, mixing colors quick
before his phrases could die like the smoke
above gray seas of laughing faces, faces of the deaf
adrift on a thousand lost dance floors.

When seizures and the shakes accompanied
those sacred *flashes*, he worked on to lengthen them
through a whole piano suite of shadow, glare,
bathtub gin, the D.T.'s, and broken light
on any borrowed uprights he could find.
Shading himself from morning stabs of sun,
he got back to where he was going all along,
the dreaming mind, the diamond-making *dark*. †

In the Dark

Drop to the dark, the deep cool and quiet, where insight
catches what a child or a blind prophet sees,
dreamed from behind the eyes.

Drift now, and imagine, here in the dark,
in the black that was here before time was,
uninterrupted by glare
of all colors locked within it, drift.

If you kneel at Our Lady of Perpetual Darkness,
you won't see the black light of candles lit by grief —
or by wonder — except under tightly shut lids.
Close the eyes. Now feel the touch

of a soft black wind that reminds you:
darkness is the darkest of rivers,
flowing underneath the earth, breathing
under skyscrapers, cornets, under our shoes,

swelling in waves along the arteries
to every idea or song ever made. Now
in the dark, dream from behind your eyes.
Deep below the undertow of minor chords,
inside every heartbeat, feel the darkness moving.

> *Commissioned by the Capitol Hill Choral Society of
> Washington, D.C., to be read over a piano performance
> of Bix Beiderbecke's* In the Dark

Blind Willie Johnson

From Suzanne des Cendres

The gospel bluesman remembered
flutters of the oil lamp
through bars of his crib
his mama shiny black
her red satin dress
his hunger through the smell
of rotting potatoes
shadows of men stealing
to her big bed
behind the curtain
and how she blinded him
with an angry handful of lye.

Play it, Willie,
they used to say
and he'd hug it hard
and under the night train
& cold owl singing
he'd slide those big chords
from that smooth
throbbing guitar of his
with a knife.

Up from the Borinage:
Three for Vincent Van Gogh

(1) In North Brabant, 1927,
     a Citizen Remembers Vincent Van Gogh

Here in Nuenen we still smile a little
at Vandersanden's story — the organist
in the Eindhoven kerk, next town south.
Well sir, back in the eighties, Van Gogh
had scraped together coins enough
for three of Vandersanden's lessons,
and he'd scare him like the very devil
with stops to shout out which of the notes
were green, which ochre or Prussian blue,
banging chords as though they'd rain
whole skies of purples, yellows, blacks —
and the pious organist locked the door
and blinds against him, but never knew
how Vincent, at the inn, sketched out
from memory the arcs of long, thin fingers.

Our *gek* little painter. Quite mad, you know.
The way we heard it, when down in France
near the end, he'd wear a circle of candles
in his hatband, trying to paint at night.
Maybe so. We know for sure
how here in Brabant, longer ago,
he'd suddenly break his chicken-walk
and drop to the road in a crouch, his eyes
half shut as though the sunlight hurt, and he'd
make right angles with his paint-stained hands
to frame the scenes he squinted into —

and the scenes, believe me sir, were nothing!
Ugly stuff! We all grin and hoot to think
how rich fools in London and New York
spend millions of guilders to gape at our shame.
He painted always and only these same old hovels
and tired trees and sometimes even

pale cottage weavers or twisted farmhands
in mud, doing their drudging and digging.
It got so strange, a priest from the other side,
the Catholic side of our town, would offer
to pay his shabby peasants a copper
for every time they'd refuse Van Gogh
when he asked to paint them at work.

When? Well sir, that must be when he left for Drenthe —
scrubby, peat-bogged land where the poor
(God warm them) make their huts of sod.
His letters to his father would praise their dirt,
calling it *reddish or bluish, yellowish*
dark lilac gray. Ja ja he talked queer
that way sometimes, crazy with colors.
You know that cloth the Drenthers wear?
Coarse dark blue stuff, cheap, scoured
by wind and weather? Van Gogh, fresh home
from there and swilling gin at the inn,
called it *a weave of infinite quiet.* Really.
After a while, no one would listen.
He talked sometimes to himself, they say.
Lived on *roogebrood* — black rye —
and strong tobacco. Didn't stay here long.

No no, he never belonged to Brabant.
Least of all to the sturdy Protestant
half of us that bred his line —
four art-dealer Van Goghs, rich
in big cities far away, and our firm
but duller *dominie,* his father,
who rightly threw him out. Vincent,
you know, before he painted,
also tried preaching the Word of the Lord.
But he didn't try to convert the heathen
souls of those wretches in foreign coal mines
as one of God's anointed would do.
Instead he joined them, shared his bread
and lived rat-poor like them in a shack.
So the pastors, embarrassed by his ways —

overzealous was the word they used —
sent the young man back to his father.
And the *vrouw* Ter Haar says she remembers
seeing him that year, 1880,
two miles beyond the parsonage,
freezing his hands rude red, trying
to paint a woman (not one of ours)
digging carrots from under the snow. †

(2) The Potato Eaters

Vincent Van Gogh, 1885

Something looks wrong. Five peasants sit
askew to the four-square table
which slides away in reverse perspective
into the darkness. The lamplight
holds them still, their skins like potatoes,
gnarls and knobs of brown hands
reaching into the dish of white flesh.
What rises from the dish like a prayer
is not a transcendent breath of light —
it's only steam off earthy potatoes.
The figure who breathes it in
is only a girl, and she gives us only
her back, which is wingless and dark
and blocks our seeing, or ever partaking.
As the walls close in, they sup without
communion, avoiding each other's eyes.
The instability calls us. We lean so close
we might fall into their ritual, unwelcome.

But the dark lets us in. These potato-
people cracked by sun and wind and dust
are created from the dirt dug daily
with their hands. What shines their supper
of potatoes to life and dignity is not
artistic arrangement, expressive eyes,
not the painter's spirit brushed piously in —

for Van Gogh it's sacred skin the color
of dusty potatoes sanctified by its resonance
with *blue shadow green soap and copper* alive
in all that darkness. From threads he knew
far down in the work of peasant weavers
in Brabant, he raised from black as from death
colors that bless — now it's burnt sienna,
too, vermillion, ripe grain and violet
seared in the soiled work-clothes and walls
in which we learn to rest and make our peace.

(3) Van Gogh, Talking to Himself, Echoes His Letters
while Surveying His Latest Works

Auvers-sur-Oise, July 1890

The high pitch of the light in Provence was a revelation.
Hunched too long over tight little sketches and studies,
I stretched out in Arles, learned to trust quick strokes
of palette knife and brush, slashes that leap and follow
each other fast, the way words do in the letters I write.
Painting isn't artifice — it's cautious lives that are,
all that planning and doubt holding back the creating.
So I don't judge God for the wild world He made — His world
is only *unfinished, a study that didn't come off.*
I try to finish creation by painting it.
And what serenity in the work! Dabbing day and night
till the brush drops out of my hand, it's not the attacks
I fear anymore, it's the lulls between the attacks.
Not to work is now the only terror I know.

Ja, but the colors I splashed in Provence distracted me.
Now I'm going for depth. Look at them, man,
I tell myself, the new ones on these walls:
that wheat those plains of lonely yellow, flinging lights
against those darkened skies slashed deep —
these new ones *hold their calm in the catastrophe.*
This last self-portrait, too — I'm the cheapest model in France —
my losses lie *quiet and vague.* Now Theo

can trash that boyish sermon of mine he saved —
I've almost finished making a parallel world
for that "Stranger in the Earth" I preached about,
sorrowful yet always rejoicing.

Theo. Faithful brother. Numskull! Alms-giving savior
ashamed of my rags and the whore I sheltered, and *ja,* Theo —
damn his eyes — the cautious dealer in art and *cold respectability*
who's blind to what I show him of how color works,
who admires my paint but keeps it out of the market,
as *ashamed* of its newness as of its eccentric maker.
Ten years of his fifty francs a month allowed me to work.
True to myself I work to betray the traitor who loves me.

Well damn anyway this talk of money. *It's like someone singing
out of tune, or as if you're pursued by a malevolent
barrel organ,* so much wheeze and chatter in the inns
and streets. . . . In that blur two years ago, after the quarrel
with Gauguin, I madly thought what to do when my ear offended me.
My eye, thank God, stays always steady on paint taking shape —
and now new images hum down low and deep as well as high,
sweating light up from the dark like the coal miners' lamps
in the Borinage I can't forget. Must tell Theo again —
black's a color! *Colour de profundis.* My palette darkens
to set the whole scale singing. Those olive groves I sent him,
the trunks are wringing blue rust green right out of the black
of their bark, I can paint as workers or weavers would paint
if they could, those souls I'd still reconcile to their lives
in and under the earth as I sit with them in the dark.

That burst of sunflowers I painted at Arles
ought to have always hanging next to it
what's opposite and yet equivalent — these cypresses.

Well, *something yet to be done.* In this *mood of almost
too much calm,* I still may find my self by losing it
in a whole landscape balanced by dark greens and blacks —
by making its *bituminous dark* (Oh miners of Borinage)
flash out softly as I blast it quickly in. . . . †

The Car in the Snow

Poetry is like prayer in that it is most effective
in solitude and in times of solitude as, for example,
in the earliest morning.
                              Wallace Stevens

She transmutes the scene of this late afternoon
into how it will look in the pre-dawn dark,
when the only visible car will hum
so softly from so far away
it will be more imagined than heard.

The snow is falling heavy enough
so she won't know the strain of the car's
yellow lights working through the drifts.
She'll see the lit-up tops of fresh-plowed banks
at the corners, and then the easy sweep of light
across white fields to the north
out past the sleeping town.

She stages it to be four a.m., when no one's up.
That's only a stranger passing through,
she will say to herself, and can pray it's not
please Lord this time not one of them,
not someone from the village sick or in trouble.
All she knows of the world at four a.m.
is what she feels by praying towards it.

She has produced this light-show,
projected it onto her fading upstairs window,
a few times before — always and only
when her own reflection is a film overlay
that wavers darkly in the glass
while heaven's snow gathers behind it,
covering edges, rounding out the town.

Now she brings from her backlit kitchen
her supper and tea on the blue Dalton china.
The prayer is finished. She will drowse

at the window as the blurred streets go faint
until, from behind car headlights, she makes out
the sudden slice of a road that opens wide
into the deep pine forests north, into at last
the dreaming dark that has been drawing her
out beyond the town, out where she's never been.

Assignment Nicaragua, 1985

The girl asked the stranger
"Why don't you come in?
The fire is lit at my place."
The wanderer answered, "I'm a poet,
I only want to know the night." †

Pablo Antonio Cuadra

(1) Easing Down toward Nicaragua

Christmas week, 1984, Isla Mujeres, Mexico

To keep from burning I've leaned
my white back against a white fishing boat
that's belly-up on the shore.
A red stripe runs under its gunwales
above *El Niño Jesus* hand-lettered in green.

A stone's throw off shore in another boat
a Mayan untangles his nets and eats his lunch.
His triangular face is like those faces I see
every morning at dawn, the clay-brown open faces
of the island children gathering in the church,

each child using only eyes at the crèche
as they play untended, play with sheep
and angels, awaiting the baby. They never touch.

I avoid the fisherman's eyes as each of us
squints now and then across the water to Cancún.
He has probably sometimes taken the little ferryboat
to see that *gringo* place of apartments and hotels
that buries the shore he knew ten years ago.

Now there's no dune grass, dust, or graves, no church,
no square where people sit under trees with ices
or coffee in that biggest town he ever saw.

Somehow now we manage a childlike talk.
His parchment face is ancient parables.
We pay out line to each other lightly
as he slits behind the gill of a grouper a quick
bright string of blood. He sells fish, he says,

only here on the island, only to the *Café La Peña.*
That's the one café I'm drawn to,
especially early morning. It faces
the shaded square and the church where the children
daily wait for *El Salvador Jesus* to be born.

He washes down some bread by draining his cup
and as he refills it I want him to offer me bread
and wine, I'm almost kneeling, terrified that he might.

(2) Assignment Nicaragua

January 1985

The poet part of me didn't come down to this revolution
smart with Spanish, furnished with data and insights
that made me special. I came here tongue-tied,
stunned by the scene of our national nightmare crime.
I walk Managua and the villages hungry for sense,
a beggar embarrassed to show the tin cup beating
under his shirt more than I'm fearful
of Contra raiders stealing down from the hills.

I know less of the techniques of terror
than of its smell (it's not the reek
behind the butcher's on a hot Sunday night,
any cameraman can make that up, it's damp rope
and the pungency of oil fumes in sour dust).
I am eyes and ears like yours, you who also distinguish
the drugged TV presentations from the sock of the hymns
these people sing to the Jesus alive in their suffering faces.

And if I jump ahead of your eye to note,
for example, that windows are full of dark
on just one side, and you've never seen that,
come anyway. Such things are not enigmas
but only the distracted moments
worth waiting for when something
(an angel, the devout *campesinos* believe)
rolls away the stone against which we usually think.

These six little poems about Nicaragua mean to serve
in the old way that poems used to serve
before we shrank our minds to the scale of newsprint
on the backsides of ads, or news as TV entertainment.
Something inside me would chant and thrum things out
at a tribal feast if I could. Now war words tighten to poems
only because, as the prophet Borges has said,
only a poem knows how to distrust the language.

(3) Managua in the Thirteenth Year after the Earthquake

1985

Managua is huddles of crating-boards between masonry ruins
that stick up out of fields that have swallowed their streets.
Street signs of the Revolution on the shacked-up boulevards —
Carlos Fonseco, Sandino, Nineteenth July —
fail to tie these barrios into a city.

Managua is the time it takes heart to knock down and rebuild
the broken blocks, which is longer than forever,
it is every day. Managua is every day.

Managua is earthquake relief in *Guardia* bank accounts in Miami,
it is deeds of the poor foreclosed by guns on Somoza's desks.
Its violence is sanctioned by the U.S. as empty shelves,
fear, the soft hands of the *campesino* driven down from his fields,
the hospital locked and emptied for lack of lightbulbs.

Managua is a warped guitar in a window, only two strings left,
Managua is a young man absently crossing himself
as he passes an empty meat hook, seeing red,

it is a locked front door framed in a field that has no homes,
it is doors of rooms suspended over the streets,
hanging rooms of colored walls with doors that cannot open
back to anywhere that anyone would care to go back to.

(4) "San Carlos Potable Water"

This project is a symbol of the cooperation
and an expression of the cordial relations between
the Republic of Nicaragua and the United States of America.

Bronze text from the 1930s on a broken cement
obelisk fountain, San Carlos, Nicaragua

Against disfigured cement
sticking out of dry ground
a wrist of broken-off pipe.
No hand can be imagined,

and there's no one in the village
who remembers far back or ever
a stream of water here
or a tin cup on a chain.

Maria Concepcion, age 4,
knew about a cup
mostly the shape she made
with her own two hands

under the squeak of the pump
behind the store of Señor Cruz.
She was one of five little ones
in San Carlos village

died of diarrhea, 1977,
thirsty at the shore of a lake.
This country where the poor
hold out their names like hands.

Eight years of wind and sun obscured
the nail-scratched names — Luz, two Pedros,
a Juan, Maria — from scraps of wood
that cross themselves on sticks to beg
the mercy of *Jesus* when He comes.
The scraps go to dust, will leave no trace —

no dates for yet another year
in which they begged Him to hurry.

But the crumbs of broken cement, spread
like mock bread, are the throat's dry cry
that starts again the old song of hope,
hope against history. The bronzed plaque fails
to lower the uplifted mother-face on the bench,
and the poetry caught in the names of children
asleep in the arms of their native dust
rises and flows from a deeper, angrier fountain.

(5) Too Quickly

January 21, 1985, Matagalpa, Nicaragua

A darting of sparrows
starts up, then
threads itself thin

and long through a seam of air
that a star might trace
when it is late and darker.

That's what she saw,
the child leaving the cotton mill,
call her Maria,

I'm sure she saw it, but now
she decides too quickly
how this hemline of sky

stitched by a shuttle of wings
comes apart with as little meaning
as the only streetlight for miles

that explodes in the tin can she kicks
through the darkening alley, eyes down,
fists deep in her pockets.

(6) Hearing the Nighttime Crowing of Cocks

Matthew 26

The cocks here don't hold back till dawn
they crack the still night air
outside this dark little church
where twelve *yanquis*
fitfully struggle for sleep
on the concrete floor,

and for every cock shriek
that cuts its way in
I start to count three ways
we have denied this *Jesus,*
this *hay-soos* whose house this is.
But shiny in Contra ammo belts
every U.S. bullet in those hills
denies that we know the man.

The ravaged villagers in whose
faces and hands
we thought we saw Him
are still asleep.
At daybreak they once again
will easter themselves
with smoke and tortillas
in front of the shacks.

What we should do is rise at dawn
and beg from these country poor
in Jesus' name, señora,
but the shine of our silver cups
would betray us, and we know
it's us and our denials
against whom the cocks are crowing.

*With the Witness for Peace delegation in Pantasma village,
to document a third raid by the U.S.-armed Contras, January 1985*

Travel Advisory

Remind yourself, when you wake to a strangeness
of foreign lights through blowing trees
out the window of yet another hotel,
that home is only where you pretend you're from.
What's familiar sends you packing,
watching for "some lost place called home."
You're from wherever you go.

Don't admit what you're looking for.
If you say to a baker in Bremen, to a barmaid
in Provence, "Back home we think of you here
as having deeper lives," they'll shrug you wrong
and won't respond. And then you'll know:
they're strangers too. Broken and wrinkled
stones and skin, brush strokes and chords,
old streets and saints you've read about,
flute-notes in the laughter of foreign children,
the nip of a local market cheese —
there's a life we almost knew once.
Watch. Just let it in.

The return ticket will take you only
to the town where you packed to get on the plane.
It never missed you. You'll notice
alien goods in your kitchen, wind in a wall,
losses in the middle drawer of your desk.
Even there, *the strange* is the cup of communion
you drink; that dim outlandish *civitas dei*
you're a citizen of never was a place.
Remember not to feel too much at home.

In the Red Sea: Snorkeling off Basata

All one needs to do is follow the sound of water,
and the persons of water, to find one's way home again,
wherever home may be.

James Wright

I

After a while you stay afloat with ease
by lazily stretching into the way things are.
You slow down to half the surfbeat of your heart.
Your knees and elbows soften and fold,
as though you had inhaled them, leaving
a vague wet lacy sensation of webs
where fingers and toes had been.
Devolving, you no longer stay on top
by kicking and splashing, you dart straight on,
one long muscle parting the realm that opens
to let you in. The law of this realm
won't let you drop. The salinity that holds you
afloat is constant, the surrounding desert
having neither rivers nor rains
to dilute this meaning of the way things are:

you have drifted to a time before we learned
to breathe on land, before the Creator's long design
opened our faces to air and we gasped to seize it.
You fight off the human instinct to open the mouth
for breath, you bite down on the snorkel's mouthpiece
to keep its seal. You can feel the seas divide
as the long lines of your cells unwind
toward their origin. From down very deep
in your self, words swim up and cleanse that vision
that those King James words just half awakened
when they tried to catch the strangeness of
in the beginning, face of the deep,
and there was light. Now, open your eyes.

II

Here shimmer displaces sound, here even water loses
its lowest whisper. That first white flash is shot
from a school of angelfish in the shape of laughter.
"As the eye sees, the body slows," a dancer told me once,
and I am undulation of water flowing,
a world away from the ticking of my watch,
which is wrapped up dry in a towel back on shore.
The tracings of desert winds are swirls
of sand along the sea-floor, under the hushed
kneeling and rising of blue xenia coral
and the mute wavings of green sea-fans.
My snorkel over my shoulder thrusts a gesture,
a blue middle finger dismissal of the war "Desert Storm"
piling up obscenely in the sands to my east
as I shoot, unarmed and wingless,
over the valleys and woods of a parallel life.

Every living animal coral down there is a home;
the reefs are towns of piled-up pastel houses
like miniature Valparaisos — but these are towns
we only dream, *civitate,* republics of mind
and heart, designed not to oppress and devour —
these are cities that feed themselves to their tenants,
to the nibbling sponges and mollusks, to fish you see
exploding like flung jewels, shooting like rockets
into the holiday night of a possible world.

III

Ignoring the deadly fire coral
as something not quite real and for later thought,
I drifted over a reef that was waving silken
scarves, purple of amethyst lapping the folds
of a woman's throat. And I forgot:
these are wrinkles from which death strikes,
forgot about lionfish, slash, soldierfish, and then,
when the ancient stonefish hurtled toward me,
I remembered triggerfish, gun, *kill,*
crashed through a whole eleventh plague of shadows

and streaks, scattered bones, flying fragments
of shells, sea bottom strewn with olive-drab husks
of army trucks lying stuck the previous night
in the Sinai — and then in heaving oily waters,
mouth agape, choking, I thrashed my fins my regrown arms
and legs like a frightened child, lunging for air, praying
for a dry path across, beating through oil,
polyps purple bruises on bombed white flesh
floating hugely toward me. . . .

IV
How heavy behind the shore.
Upright to the land and its brown breathing,
lugging hard, I lurched off-balance,
squinting dizzy in the blinding sand,
tripping over flippers, lungs afire,
shoved from behind by this demand
that I must walk but wanting only
to lie down, to stretch, to retract,
unwind, to slither back to water
the way a sleeping child, his covers kicked off
by a dream on a winter night, grasps for the quilt —
risking another nightmare, suspended,
eyes closed tight, hoping he's home. †

December 27-28, 1990

A Sighting

We watched this old gray boxcar lumber past
the crossing, the name *Roscoe, Snyder, and Pacific*
almost washed away — and hey, I said, look,
a first name a last name and a sea,

but Gordon, who loved sighting trains even then,
with his last chance for a little luck fading fast,
slowly said his only poem ever

as he watched what he knew was there.
No, he said — eyes scanning the track
the way the train had gone — no, it's just
two little towns in Texas and a dream.

In memory of Gordon Darrah

Ending the Nationwide Poets' Strike

We were badly organized, Zimmer.
Our poets' strike wheezed through night streets
here and there for months
like a punctured lung.
Maybe six thousand poets closed shop,
and nobody noticed.
Even if the thousands of scabs —
poets who've given up reading —
had gotten the word and joined in,
it might not have mattered much.
We're mostly night shift anyway,
moonlighters. There are few other persons

awake enough to assess the national losses:
words so close to death that buzzards
circle and squawk where poets should;
novelists blocked and weeping; Tom Wolfe
sticking 2,343 exclamation points
into a single book to prick words alive;
the union finding a team willing to count them.

There are reports of a shortage of rhythms,
and of wine going sour in vats. Candles
are scarce. People are returning flutes and
paintings and snowstorms, demanding refunds.
Next they're going to believe fat speeches
from the Senate. In your steady Iowa, under
the gray Old Testament sky, plastic lawn ornaments
in 24% of the yards for heaven's sake.
We poets cannot let this go on.
It's time to send out the word:
break up the lines, get back to work.
We've made them suffer enough. †

For Paul Zimmer

Proposing the Text for a United States National War Memorial

April 2003

Poets work to shape a homeland
where just a few lines on a stone
would get it right forever,
the way the dead themselves
might talk, no orations pillars or pomp,
a few lines in simple form
to cut their way into
the national memory.

But art just now comes in last.
Now as we're rushed to a new war
and are asked to salute an overwrought
memorial to an old one,
I can only try to flash awake
the screens of a few thousand monitors
with four lines by James Agee
that the politicians would have us forget:

> We soldiers of all nations who lie killed
> Ask little: that you never in our name
> Dare say we died that men might be fulfilled.
> The earth should vomit us against that shame. †

A Disquisition upon Whistling

(1)
My summer neighbor, the Lost Valley
dulcimer maker, whistles to the wood he works
until the wood is fit for its strings.

(2)
That old phonograph record
"The Whistler and His Dog"
had a catchy tune whistled so well that the dog
always rewarded his master at the end
with exactly three barks, pausing before the third.
Amazed at how they always got it right,
I'd again wind up Uncle Charley's Victrola.

(3)
I grew toward people who whistled at work
and to and from work, then listened evenings
on their family radios for the trills of Elmo Tanner.

(4)
And in high school we played that jukebox record
of Bob Haggert whistling through his teeth, air
leaking out all over, "Big Noise from Winnetka." 1941.
Impossibly wispy and ghostly, that little blues
struggling through the spaces between real notes —
maybe it's what silenced thousands of whistlers,
even for a while Bing Crosby. Or was it

(5)
how the big war came marching through
blowing shrill police whistles,
leaving behind it streets and streets of silence.

(6)
An interruption and an echo.
At dawn one morning in 1948, a stranger
walked up Prince Street past my college digs,
whistling Sousa as stridently
as our milkman in the thirties ever did.
Apple-cheeked and cheery, plump
as an ad for the yellowy milk he pulled
by barnlight from his whistle-clean cows,
glass chiming in his wire basket
like a wayward glockenspiel, Mr. Bussies
would puff up and down the banks
in front of our houses, along our driveways,
whistling through snow or summer dew,
whistling down my sleep or up
to my waking, marching the four left-rights
up our back stoop, whistling Sousa, rousing
us to keep step in a world we almost believed in.

(7)
Real whistlers go it alone. I read somewhere how
the rag-tag volunteers at the Boston Tea Party, 1773,
were led up the side of one of the ships
by George Robert Twelves Hewes, a lowly shoemaker.
No uniform, no braids or epaulets, a man well known
on the waterfront, but only for his whistling.
How well revolutions understand it: you need
a whistler, not drums and a big brass band
when the needed and narrow way is hard to find.

(8)
If grandchildren come to visit
in the summertime, I will just happen
to lead them to look for berries
very close to where they can hear
the dulcimer maker whistling.

For Curt Sanders, Lost Valley Dulcimers

Hats and Awnings

Driving through Holland, Michigan, 1999

As I wait for the light to change,
people in dark clothes tumble and swirl
through water beads and little rivulets
in my outside rearview mirror.
All of them, men and women, are wearing hats.
As I race my idling engine, staring in,

one gray hat breaks through like the sun
bobbing down River into the clearing weather
on Main. Under dripping tan awnings,
vaguely familiar, which are everywhere now
in the mirror, a blur of white hand rises
and tips the hat, tips it high skyward

above blue eyes, and the step beneath it
brightens to pick up an oldie hit song.
The music is not out there — it's my car radio
dubbing it into the scene with an old recording
that sings, *Tonight the world is gonna be mine.*
It is Nineteen Thirty Five and it is my father,

together he and the year slide off from my mirror,
slip into Keefer's for a nickel cup of coffee.
He's planning. Our family is on its way out,
to be strangers in other towns. The horns
that snarl and honk behind me are cheering us on
as I let up on the clutch and move through the light.

Truant Dancer

While the smart set in our ninth-grade class
spent Monday nights in Miss Cream's Dancing School,
laughing and learning together the fox-trot
under the big-mooned music of Vaughan Monroe,
I would sneak off to Drake's for cokes,
free from the fear that I'd stumble left-footed
into the roundy soft and firm of angora sweaters.

Two solid hours squared off in a wooden booth
toward the back, with Spotty and Phil and Dorf,
guys from St. Thomas High who lived downtown
from our Burns Park social life. Over Krupa's drums
from the jukebox, we'd worry about the Tigers
with Gehringer gone. Our only stylish move
was the worldly squint, like Humphrey Bogart's,
the little rhythm in passing around a glowing Lucky.

Drake's was four blocks of ache away
from just how the pretty girls could turn,
tilt a little, spark their eyes
and sigh as they felt boys pull them close
in the "box step," 1 and 2 and 3 and,
and then release them for the "open walk,"

that part of the fox-trot I mastered all alone,
feet turned in, left arm extended,
right arm embracing the air, gliding
from the last streetlight to our porch light
(making up the scent of stars and her hair)
coming home with another false report
on my weekly dancing class.

Herm Klaasen to Himself

Spring is no longer a verb for how we get up
out of chairs to answer the door — spring we don't.
Those springtime tweets aren't birds, they're electric
squeals when we try to tune in to the world,

and red gets into our dreams three times
as *stop* or blood or ambulance lights
for every time it is coals on a windy beach,
or a woman's dress, or valleys of shining apples.

The phone rings less. Letters are shaky and few.
This walk to friendly coffee gets longer; right now
you stop to remember again (third time this week)
that Bert closed his coffee shop down. Keep going:

with slower steps there's more past to be seen.
No fences, so the milkman wades through snow to where
your mom hung sheets with bluing in them, and *flap*
it's autumn snap right through the hot metal stink

of traffic near the graveyard where she is.
Forget the coffee, you'd have to drive to the mall,
where nobody's there by the hundreds. Remember,
getting home, turn north where the butcher was,

skinny old what's-his-name. You can't find a soul
who knows half the world you see! So now, Hermie
boy, you can start that reel again in your head
from yesterday — the graceful couple

raisin-wrinkling among us (one of them you)
shy again as they slowly undressed in the dark.

This Way Out

His skin hangs loose "but shrivels," he says —
"look here, where it puckers and darkens."
He grins to call himself "a slowly leaking balloon."
You see lines dancing about his mouth and eyes.
He eases shut a heavy burgundy book
and announces quite grandly, "The lamps
behind my eyes have the wicks down low,
and not much oil left." Head angled high
he cuts an eye toward your response,
hears it perfectly from across the room,
but even so leans forward, cups a gnarled hand
behind his ear to catch your praise.
He calls you sonny. You're sixty-six.

The nurse says he begs each night,
as children do, to "stay up a little longer."
The tapioca has sagged to gruel,
untouched, but he's on his third cup of coffee,
hot and black. "After dark," the nurse has told you,
"he hums a lot," and you hear the humming
begin, steady deep notes of old Dutch psalms,
sounded just when you're out of things to say
and your lapses tell you that it's time to leave.
You know he'll hum and hum with nothing to hum to
except the whole strange world out past the glass
dimming to night across the hospital's parking lot,
where your headlights will narrow down to a beam
that scans the darkness for that sign, *This Way Out.*

Frisian Psalms, 1930s

When the gray of winter afternoons
howled bible black into Friesland's nights
and the windows one by one
made yellow squares along the iced canals
beyond the village, one farm stayed dark
longer than the rest. Some said it was just
to save kerosene, but that wasn't it.

In that house, Fridsmas', the *mem* would call
into shadows from the little reed organ
crammed in the kitchen, "Children, come —
we will sing some psalms." It would teach them,
she said, to be unafraid in the dark
before coming through to the cheer of the light
to see by, when it would come.

For Douwe Tamminga

Still . . .

Later Poems, 2005-2010

The Function of Poetry at the Present Time

When you see
an old shoe
at the side of a road
there is never a second shoe.
Someone has to notice.

Window

He looks skyward and sees he forgot
to snap off the lamp in his upstairs study.
He'd call it aging, but aging is not, he tells himself,
a downward slope. He hadn't climbed to get here,
his life isn't a hill. It's more like a long sleep,
with tens of thousands of dreams, dreams of colors
and pathos, love and loss, humor and terror.
A dream that Someone Else had been having about him,

he wonders if that's what took him here to his mid-morning
cup of coffee in the little walled patio, noticing
Mrs. Czarnecki's roses, those fat pink ladies' fists
shaking gently over the wall between them.

He feels the morning sun and is drowsy again,
like that droning bee, cloyed and woozy
in the sweet-smoke fumes of its blue work,
fumbling the skirts of the morning glories.

It's alright that everything is young and new —
even the oldest books up there in his study,
dark in their bindings. They've changed their minds
because the world around them has changed —
as the best books always knew it would change.
Nothing is wrong if the book he brought down
slips from his lap and claps the patio bricks, once again
startling him to the high wonder of where he is.

Early Retirement: A Note Left at the Office

I've quit. I want
to be outside before
a woman's call
that echoes through twilight
says it's time for bed.
I want to play out
a little longer.

Give the Unfinished Projects file to Plumly.

Falling Down

We do it as toddlers
and again when we are old.
Downward is the right direction,
the metaphysical pull
toward reality, grounding us, knowing
that skyward flight is for the birds.

Say falling is a kind of practice
for humanity's last descent, bones to earth,
bones learning to listen for the one note,
refusing the delusion of ascent.

We'll respect the concrete
(where we sometimes fall)
for being concrete, not abstract.
Eyes downward, we take it slow, wary of
pratfalls, knowing the truth of down, and still
keeping our feet on the ground.

Thick Lenses

Dimming down, their wicks sputtering low,
how eager the eyes of the octogenarians
to crack open the layer of tissue
thickening over a printed page or over
a painted landscape, how they wish
to brush aside slight snows
out the frosted window,
to dab color into fading faces,
and like Milton to stare
with clean recognition
into worlds they may never yet have seen.

For Tom Harper

Peacock Sighted against
a Bright Background of Snow

As he spreads and flashes his tail, I look
into its thirty staring eyes unfurled and remember
they are to be seen but see nothing — distractions
evolved in the glacial light of ice-age winters
to lure hens and scare off half-wit predators.

I think I see directly his blazings
of hot copper, icy teal, green, red, blue.
I don't. He carries no pigments,
only reflections from little unseen bubbles —
optical interference phenomena

is how science classifies this miracle
of colors that move and change. I circle
around him to catch the display from every angle,
and my eyes, blinded by light, absorb again
the assurance of something unseen.

Civilization

Archaeologists in China have found the world's
oldest playable musical instrument — a 9,000-year-old
flute carved from the wing bone of a crane.

Los Angeles Times

Long before Greeks measured to mark
the frets on their lutes, dividing tight strings
by exactness of tones, long before that,

someone in China, probably a girl with time
and some need to walk alone near the sea,
lifted to lips the hollow wing bone of a crane

and blew through it, no thought of why,
mixing sky-air that lifts wings and sleeves
with the unseen source of life they called breath.

Imagine the whistles and arcing bird-cries
these people learned to make as they breathed
through bones with scaled apertures and lengths

and drilled little holes where fingers could find
the tunes beyond birdsong they began composing.
How plaintive and lonely the wordless sounds

must have been as they called out thin, rose, then
drifted into and through the Bo leaves, over rocks,
or hung like clouds of smoke in rafters, then

vanished as softly as morning mist off the Yangtze,
thoughts half-remembered. But the tunes lacked
grounding, lacked sounds that tied light melodies

down to stone floor and soil and the warm flesh
of hands. Centuries later, long miles westward,
high up in Greece and getting out of the wind,

chapped hands of shepherds and goatherds tugged
animal guts and dried them and learned to snap
their lengths of string to vibrate them

against flat wood, later hollowed out,
to resonate the deeper tones for love or despair
that Athenian throats would sing if only they could.

The sweaty pluck and thrum of finger and hand
hefted earth sounds upward, rising to meet
the vibrato of long breaths ringing out of

that hollow wing-bone, and the melding created
dialogue, Greek harmony, music, compassion,
a transcendence of selves, a republic.

Automat

Edward Hopper, oil on canvas, 1927

Nothing automatic or newly modern here, nothing springs open
to dispense a bowl of hot soup or a cool slice of pie
in exchange for coins. But neither will a waiter intrude.
The young woman sits alone, fashionably dressed and
without expectation. Surely someone said he would meet her,
but that was at another place, and hours ago. The round
white table top repeats its cold infinity in a small empty dish.
The chair across from her is hopelessly tight to the table,
and her left hand is already — or still — in its glove.

In the dark window looming behind, the thirteen ceiling lights
are only reflections, they disappear out there in a curve
of distance. The window sill's a proscenium for yawning spaces
on either side, and it holds only a single overfilled bowl
of glass bananas and apples. Almost unnoticed in the outside
dead of night is the one window in all New York that's lit.
It's blue. That dab of paint is the cosmos breaking through
the canvas, a universal ache that brushes Hopper's
numbed woman seated alone in a spare interior
where everything is a set, where nothing can act by itself.

For Cathy Kopikian

Reading Faces

Slowed down by the snow storm, mesmerized
by the heartbeat swish of wipers on windshield
brushing away the flakes, I drifted into old thoughts
of my father — teacher, physician, student of faces —
his respect for his alcoholic patients, each of the hundreds,
tender toward their long thirst for a home
that strives in vain to displace the only home we know.

Addiction, he said, *is 80 to 100 proof that spirit exists,*
and that it craves to be incarnate, to be flesh.
But he saw how it sometimes runs in reverse,
the body craving spirit, fixing some drinkers onto
highly distilled escapes from the world of matter,
looking for what's disembodied and timeless.
Not his world. He took his incarnation straight, no fizz.

I'm home after a stop at Gallagher's
for fish & chips and a beer. Retired,
I could of course spend one more evening
reading the morning paper. But my furnace
rattles gray like death, takes my mind's heartbeats
down the hall that goes nowhere but out, out across
towns and faces making tracks across morning papers.

Christ, resurrected as lowly among us,
something has to stop our news from becoming home,
these faceless bombings, slogans, genocides, our escapes
with thrusting rockets and needles into fleshless non-worlds.

What a whited and cold sheet of paper I am,
here at my desk making these tracks, thinking the masks
of the usual 5:15 daily gang at Gallagher's bar,
each weary face as severely its own
as the labels on bottles that reverse the mirror,
imprinting for some the only good news for now.

Reading faces and trying to trace our escapes, I learn,
learn that words matter like the bodies

of spirit that words really are, learn again
what my father learned — not to look up in the sky
for some wispy, mere spirit godkin Christ,
or some fiery avenger, but down
the lost faces where the Word-made-flesh lives,
because He cannot be abstract words,
dead print in a black book, ink on the bleached
morning papers, or His faceless tracks in the snow.

Credence

Is seeing believing?
The dog that bit me when I was eight
had the white silky hair of the angel
I had seen sometimes next to my bed,
the same soft, gentle eyes.
She offered love with a big
floppy paw. Nice doggie.
I got four stitches, a bandage,
a tetanus shot, and the gift of doubt.
I thought about it later in college:
Cogito ergo sum? Dubito ergo sum.

But the mix of thinking and doubting
didn't answer shadows or tow my mind
up to its snowline; it walled out the reality
of low-lying mists and hidden clues to wonder.
I learned I could know more than I see.
I learned I could see more than I know.
Who knows why all bubbles create and hold
the same predestined shape? Who isn't amazed
to learn how an infant creates and files
her lifelong insights while playing out
little sounds called words?

Once, as close ago as forever, in an Iowa village
that branded with smeared yellow paint
the houses of young men deferred from the draft
for a war in an anywhere called Korea, I watched
my friend Sietze — teacher today, boot camp tomorrow —
watched his face transfixed in wonder as he listened
with his mind's ear to the chords of a Bach cantata —
simply by seeing printed notes while turning pages.
Beyond spite and waving flags, past even the set
grindstones of doctrines, the surprise of joy can slip in,
alive, still astride the realities of discord and death.

There must be a final music: I think it must be
stemmed in a glass of red wine, its rim ringing

under the coarse rub of a finger, humming
the harmony of long-pending chords,
the clash of variant notes resolved, resolved.
It swells and swirls the liquid of its lyric
even where the solid creeds force arguments
with abstractions — *reconcile, savior, communion,
forgiveness* — a flow that raises us from our knee bones
clapping and swings us along all the way
into a strange poem that's called, yes, *forgiveness.*

Video quia credo. Credo quia absurdum est.

Texts for Three Needlepoint Samplers

Make Sun
While the Hay
Shines.

A Stitch in Time
May Close
a Stunning
Revelation.

You Might Miss It.
Leap
Before You Look.

I'm Only Human

I'm only human, as the man said who deep inside himself
refuses to believe it . . .

Dylan Thomas

The scent of curry with ginger root, even in winter,
sends from nose to mind a hot August morning of tennis
with incongruous church bells ringing cold.
What stirs this — maybe a broiled haddock on a plate —
doesn't matter much. So waiters sigh and look away
while I wander off to wonder if such skips through time & space
just might mean I'm born to be some kind of seer. Forget it.

There's the time I sat in Cleveland's airport and tried to think
why I shivered as I left the plane, hurrying past a sign
that said *Your Exit May Be Behind You.* Deep in thought,
I missed my connection, and mislaid the reason
for going back to Michigan anyway. I get in trouble that way —
get lost swerving into alternatives. I wish it didn't happen.
I like guys who make mental blueprints and get all the way
home to dinner without losing them, guys who remember

numbers. I remember things like a neighborhood
spaniel barking like a seal. How my youngest son as a boy saw
minivans as buses for midgets and little stone arches
between buildings as bridges for squirrels. I started to write
my will and it became a list of good things for my wake, things
like single malt scotch. Parades and cheering embarrass me.
What it comes down to is this — I'm just not my type.

The Runaway

As I wait for the computer screen
to come on, a single light moves in
from far behind it, a pinpoint growing

larger, larger, until it lurches into place
as an old train engine filling the screen. But now
steam and station lights swirl to change it into
a school-days photo, faded to yellowish brown,
of Herky — runt in rags and got-no-pa Herky,
who died back then and none of us cared.

He is crouched and staring as always
at the big black straining engine
that twice each day pulled the cars
with shiny windows through our town
to Chicago. The engine shakes
and huffs, catching its breath, but now

Herky has vanished into the steam
so I run and run for the train's departure,
catch the handrail and swing myself
aboard, riding the clicks alone through
the night, leaving town, leaving town
to live out Herky's life and my own.

Reading a Milk Carton in a Supermarket
in My Old Hometown

Distributed by TruVal Dairy Products, Inc.
486 Woodward Ave, Detroit, MI 40237

Milk carton, Holland, Michigan

When I grew up in Holland in the thirties
the names of dairies conjured up
black-and-white cows under cool green shade
with freshets of water nearby: names like *Elm Valley,*
Lakeside, Maple Grove, Cold Spring, Beaver Dam.
At our house, *Cloverleaf* sang of tasty greens
in the cud they chewed, drowsy, swelling with milk.

A few dairy names were local I.D. cards, assuring us
that no worldly cows from elsewhere were horning in:
Holland Creamery, Tulip City. We even knew
which of our covenant heifers were calmed by peaceful views
while grazing: *Hillcrest, Riverview, Golden Vista.* Such words
when herded together, neatly lettered on trucks and bottles,
buttered the way through what parents called the Depression.

Of the fifteen dairies for our town of fifteen thousand,
only two resisted romance and took workaday names —
Consumers. Square Deal. Plain as crates and adding machines.
I like to think that they were the first to go.
One dairy — stuck on the very edge of town, being pressed
on all sides by new houses, street lights, cement —
flagged itself anyway rural as the mysterious *Rivulet Hurst.*

Our cows must have been scrubbed with Dutch cleanser.
They all had names and papers, and smiled, we imagined,
while yielding milk to their godlike farmers — our milkmen.
And all winter long, with little stand-up trucks and wire baskets,
the farmers stole in before daylight to the town's back doors or stoops
with glass pints and quarts of snow white milk, each bottle
wearing under its printed cap a rich collar of light gold cream.

In spring, we kids knew the very day the cows were sprung
from their stale winter barns and sour fodder, set free at last
to munch in the meadows. How? By the tang of new onion grass
In our glasses of milk. We talked of it at school. I liked to imagine
hundreds of cows stampeding from winter barns
and onto the singing meadows, dancing, udders flying, snorting,
snuffling up the sweet-smoke joy of born-again grass,

while — springy as hop-scotch and baseball mitts — the dawn
    sunlight
lit up again the proud little trucks with their painted names, so nice to
    say —
Cloverleaf, Maple Grove . . . ah, the fifteenth: *Meadowbrook* . . .

Marge's Thursdays, Living at Harmony Home

Many's the Monday I took the sheets back in
from rain and snow, almost dry, so white
they were tinted blue. I'd drape them from
the high cellar shelves like Ma showed me to do,
corners tucked under jars of peaches and beets.
I'd leave them in the half dark and hope
for the weather to turn. Down there, in the rich
smell of bleach and the brown soap I'd grated
and the coppery steam from our double boiler,
it's like they'd wait for me to free them again
to dance and snap and breathe alive in the wind.

So here comes Maria down the pink & lavender hall
with sheet-sets flat in plastic on her cart
that squeaks. *It's Thursday, not Monday,* I tell her again,
but here come her sheets, with their usual creases,
pasty sick white like my thighs, and breathing
not the slightest little whiff of the way Fels Naptha
could mingle with the smell of the sun and the clouds
that blew in from Lake Michigan, five miles west.
Back then rutted dirt roads kept us out, mostly, and also
high dunes, so it was deep blue water
we seldom saw, but thought a lot about it.

Attuned

In the traffic of Chinatown's market
the vendor, uncertain and tiny
next to her neat stacks of crates
that bulge with feathers and squawks,

explains why one pet cricket
in his little stick cage
is still worth more than all the others:
"Just listen to his song."

Language Formation: An Introduction

When canals were almost the only roads
by which 400 villages and a few market towns
were held together in tiny Friesland,
and the big winds off the *Mare Frisicum*
were tamed to push the brown-sailed barges
up and down through green meadows —
about the time the half-taught cartographers
were stripping history from the name
and calling it just a site, *the North Sea,*

the canal men would exchange words in passing,
phrases smuggled into each other's ports
in the mouths and bellies of returning townsmen
along with the kegs of salt herring from Wierum
to Snits, the butter and red balls of cheese
from Ljouwert to Dokkum.

The sails floated past black & white cows
lying down in green beside the still waters,
cows grouped under trees as if waiting
for a later century of Dutch landscape painters,

while the bargemen waved and talked from atop
their loads (potatoes from Bitgum, whale oil and oranges
from the seaport of Harns). Sometimes distant shouts —
at a skipper who loiters at a drawbridge while paying
his copper, or perhaps the hollered last line of a joke
from a helmsman raising his tankard — but mostly
it was gossip and news talked abruptly
over the swirling water before the flapping of sails
took them out of the range of each other's voices —

which is why Frisians even now say little, but break
their diphthongs hard, make rough consonants in the quiet
churning of vowels, every syllable swelling and ringing and
tolling as if it must make landfall, home, before fading out.

Giving It a Name

Sodden cloak that flaps
over clods and bogs
and soggy roads

but still stirs
clouded visions
out past the filmy glass —

that feathery breath
of air and faint light, that dripping veil of gray —

what old Saxons stared through
when they named this weather *fog*.

Meditation for Clarinet in Three Movements

(1)

poco agitato

Long slender rockets thrust and rip
through the starlight sheen, through veils
and spangles and flashy ribbons
that almost disguise
the ninety-five percent of existence
that is wholly blackness.
Science gets abstracted as a tangle of footnotes
while crowds cheer the next thrust
as one more conquest,
another notch in the hot warrior's belt.

(2)

calando

Stage lights over the bar
clamped high along iron beams
spill blue, yellow, and red through hot gels,
they spatter the metalsmith's tracings
mounted on an ebony clarinet
as its notes rise into the lights.
Reflections leap as fingers fly quick
to uncover and cover the silver rings
and keys. This is how one man's breath —
his spirit — throbs through tiny black holes
like the venting at the huge black center
of our galaxy — expanding, creating.

(3)

mysterioso

The clarinet meditates
soft and low as moss

a night-time stroll
down an empty shoreline,

then higher through a meadow
where starlight has stolen in

to touch, from lost
millennia, the icy glow

of a perfect lump of crystal
no one has seen

that has surfaced
in twisted grass

and the music is saying:
now we are less alone.

A Note to the Swedish Mystic Who, Writing about Laundry in the Wind, Says *"The Wash Is Nothing but Wash"*

It's here again — that late afternoon wind
off the lake. It rises up and offers
incense of lifted hot grape leaves
infusing a laundry-like steam
of wet towels and swimsuits
tossed on the vine to dry. Above, two herons,
buffeted toward inland horizons,

and now she is walking up the two-track road
from the mailbox, slowly, reading a letter.
Once again I know what's holy is not wind,
it is leaves and wet clothes, words on paper,
waves breaking off their sentences, her hair
blown across her mouth, her own way of walking.
The wind, Tommy Olofsson, is nothing but wind.

From Seaman Davey Owens' Diary, 1511

Merchant Ship Rhiannon
12th May
Still bearing southwestward

The sea wide and endless
under the creak of the boards that pull
our twisting wake through tepid waves,
with burning skin we are hurled day after day
into and out of the stare of the empty sky.

Cut loose, we follow stars through black
that curve us toward nowhere we know.
Below deck we wrestle with damp gray sleep
while the Captain whispers mad to the moon, they say,
over charts the Padre says came right from the Devil.

Back in Carmarthen, same moon,
neighbors rise now to cut and plane and square
straight beams and planks for Jenkins' mill,
and Gwynn joins the maids upstream to pick
orange flowers, yellows, and reds, to plait in their hair.

Holiday Detour to Another Neighborhood

The polished red and silver fire trucks are on show;
their engines have stopped panting

in the dark shade of Oak Street as they hold,
all set to take their places in the Fourth of July parade.

Detoured anyway from where he lives — downtown Washington —
the man parks and takes a walk. Over spangled paper hats he sees

a child's collapsed wading pool hung on the side of a house,
a smiling yellow mouth near tan, burned-out grass.

He thinks how lemonade on ice would sell right now —
which may be what a girl on the curb whispers to her cat.

Doubling back the three blocks to Ash, where his car is waiting,
he sees this time how neighbors gather on each other's porches

to chat as they listen for the band to start, and now
he can notice frosty pitchers and clinking glasses of lemonade.

No one knows that the man passing by, at least for today, is lost.

Jazz Counterpoint

On Puerto Rico's southern coast
you almost can't hear
the brushed percussion at the shore.

Those lappings like heartbeats
are hushed night and day
by the roar and crash of breakers

drumming on the rocks & reefs
just eighty feet out.
It's a rhythmic tension that

shuffles a counterpoint
no composer has caught,
but its cross-rhythms

spring to another life when
a jazz cornetist I know
tells a young student (learning

to improvise jazz) he must foot-tap
the skips and pulses inside him
in daily practice for years

so that always in U Street clubs,
his foot an obedient metronome,
his mind breaks through and back to

his own beat, his own drum, slightly
off, riding through the rift in which
the hot musical phrases can happen.

For David Jellema

Wreckers

Now we call them tow trucks.
Back when they were wreckers
if some men had a wreck or
some kind of trouble, they would call out
somehow and then a little truck with a hook
would either bring help or pull them away,
but how did the callers know which?

My father, the wrecker always
on night call in our house, would try
to bring help for my call with his flashlight —
See? No bear under the bed —
he was a scientist. I figured he didn't know
the bear comes back
as soon as the daddy leaves. I wondered

what he might say about other nighttime wreckers.
If Uncle Lym in his old Ford called out,
couldn't they wreck him, like the word says,
or hook him and pull him away to where
we couldn't find him? I never asked. Still,
I was learning. Out there among harsh streetlights
whatever answered probably wouldn't bring

a quiet voice and a glass of milk, or the kind
of chatter that came along with the flashlight.
I don't remember the night in which I first realized
that the gentle wrecker my father never hauled off
or extinguished the bear. He left it to glow and pant
and glisten again in the mystery dark of that world
he wisely allowed to be always my own to encounter.

Walking One Night Past My Hometown's Long-Abandoned Piano Factory

Out past the new streetlights, blades of a fan
in a basement window of the factory
turn slowly and slice a beam of light
from somewhere, no more beam
than a candle might make,
the blades cutting it into even measures
and laying them down in the snow.

What takes shape is a shivering
keyboard of black-and-white notes
wanting warm composition
into dark D-minor chords
for small fingers to play long ago
in the lost gas-lit parlors of our town.

The Hinge

Down the pre-dawn road that drops west from his house
to his writing shack, we'd have seen very little,
so only imagine this poet squared off at his desk,
nudging his pencil to catch the curves of the earth's lines
darkly falling away while we were hanging onto
the arcs of our own little sleeps. As one by one
the lights of barns flicked on all along the valley,
the yellow circle of his lamplight, near the old pump,
must have spread, faded to white, and then snapped off,

and it's seven now and we are up. We watch
from the kitchen window. His thermos,
a blue-flame flash, swings as he unbends
lightly toward eastern light, growing back his size.
He swaggers a little like a smithy who's forged
and polished the perfect hinge, who wears sparks
newly dead that his clothes now remember as smoke.
Full height now, he vaguely returns our waves,

but mostly he slows his step to note how the plants
that Sue had set out in April are beginning
to ignite tomatoes, green turning pink, and that Sheba
barked once and is running to meet him halfway.

Fishing Up Words in Norway

Why you ask would I try to lure a new poem
by reading classified ads from a village paper
in a country and a language I don't know? Well, first,
it was late at night, and windy. Then too, an ancient
wall clock was clicking out the seconds through the empty
bar room of the old Norse inn near Haga, and almost no lights
through branches from the huddle of houses. That's all
good prose, but how test a poem that wants to come in?

Make it stay out in the wind and ring the bell a while
as you start with what's not yet there. The first move
is on paper. Sometimes, as on that night you ask about,
I like to knock on meaningless foreign words, straining
to hear strange sounds inside their shells. Villagers
buying and selling *engangs-varer* — I'd guess that's *Norsk*
for "outgoing wares," disposables — can start it off.
Country voices break yard-long vowels on rocky consonants

— a child's bike *(jente sykkel)* or a fishing rod *(fiskestang)*,
cries out toward cast-offs — a *svaer klokke* (surely a large
heavy bell) or *gammel skjorten* (perhaps old shirts?) —
glorious junk coming to life as loudly or softly as my hunches
for meanings will permit, sounds that almost touch now and then
the pressures they hold that could make them sing.
This might be when I know I've beckoned in from the windy porch
a sprite of a poem to sit and talk as together we find it a body. †

Incident at the Savannah River Mouth

Hillybilly streams
come harping in and in
toward the sea, but
here slow down
their twang,

hold deep in the mouth
their stiller flow,
waiting in this hush
of salt hay and marsh
to slip away
whenever the moon
says *now*. Still.

Dusk and rising tide.
Guitar chords
from a far-off radio.
Through hanging mist
I can just make out
in rental boat 8
a tall figure alone.

Oars resting, crossed,
he leans with the drift
and I squint to watch
with tightening fists,
nails biting my palms,
I strain into the loosening dark
that takes him out.

About Loss

What we lose that's gone — a photo,
the year we had planned to spend in Spain,
just a minute for goodbyes with a son
who died, the many chances to prove
the love that survives its own failures —

we can get on without them.
Their absence is never the point.
Loss itself is not an absence,
its very presence is what stirs us:

the son remembered, the daughters
who couldn't make it home to their births,
the opening phrase of a poem or of music
meant to say love but can't resolve its motif.

Sometimes I catch, against green leaves
in our ancient silver maple, three seconds
of bunting flashing his indigo shape
of early morning praise that's still
almost lost and trying to break through.

Passage

Her mind misunderstood
what I meant her body to feel
those many times my hand
pressed her back
guiding her through a lobby
or onto a subway train.
Being pushed

is what she thinks
when my anxious touch
overstates
my need that we
stay connected
through closing doors and into
the loneliness of any crowd.

If I Could Paint Her

If I could paint her
I would slash my way
through this room, the painting's

foreground, catching a happy clash
of figured rug, dun and yawning wall,
and wildly florid table cloth,

brushing in a hot disorder as contrast
to her in the middle distance.
The white chair near the left edge

almost washes out to a delusion.
The small rooster framed on the opposite wall
sheds flakes of teal and copper everywhere

as she comes into focus just beyond,
seated on a balcony
under a red umbrella, breathing,

and she slowly takes on flesh tones
from the room as its colors change.
I make the sea in the background

strain to heave its way into the frame
in which she is very still, body at the brink
of swaying, her eyes holding the after-image

of having been downcast, disappointed,
even as they look up, startled by the recognition
of how and why a would-be painter loves her.

For Michele

Appearance and Reality

I've read how new cameras can slender
their baggy overweight subjects,
can even make old skin smooth as petals
by erasing its blotches and wrinkles.
Thus we make obsolete the signals
the aging body presents.

But while we refine our "looks,"
clicking our shiny photos away
to distant addresses for praise, and
posting our descendants a spread
of ancestors, us, for framing on future walls —

our mirrors, unliberated slaves,
daily force us to that weary question
raised by Plato and F.H. Bradley —
How tell the appearance from the real? —
dragging us back to pre-technology.

We can't, like red-nosed Elizabeth the First,
order all mirrors removed, ignoring simple optics.
But with *through-a-glass-darkly*-type thinking
displaced, we're assured that we've rid ourselves
of the old philosophical problem — we are
apparently no more than what we appear to be.

Dark Glass: Four Poems

(1) Breath

Bath Abbey, England, 1509

It's Thomas I'm called, sir, and as you see
by the scorched apron, glassmaker by trade.
In truth how we learned glassblowing
is only by what comes down
through the holy stories you know.
We make glass from inside us, y'might say,
by easy breathing of creator-breath
or "spiritus" some call it. We breathe windows to life
out of small rivers of steaming color
by stirring impurities into the light —
the alchemists' powders of iron, cobalt, copper —
all earth-stuff, that's what pure glass lacks,
dirt as dead as the dust Adam came from.

'Zounds, sir, what's it all for? Something o' this:
when folk come inside it's from the west door they come,
so it's dark, dark like a cave, like a womb,
it's the womb of Our Lady. The windows
pull folk into dreams, say the priests, to dream
the whole Book from right where they stand,
dream of God creating the world from black,
dream Jacob and the angel, Our Lord and the Saints.
Dream is what master painter tells us to make in glass.

So the colors we blow, score, and bind, it's said
they make what's holy become real and right here —
the wild spears of sunlight they catch from the sky —
catch the same way, you see, as how
the dust could catch and keep God's breath
when He made our father Adam,
catch the same way the Eucharist
grabs and holds onto the Spirit whelming inside
the reds and purples of swollen grapes.

(2) Catching Light

Shelley's flight into abstractions, pursuing
his shining Spirit far past all time and earth,
blinded him to think that life itself
like a dome of many-colored glass,
stains the white radiance of eternity.

But look: just stand in a dim cathedral,
holding your gaze as tourist cameras click
around you, and see how the colors
give to the light streaming in from out there
not stain but the very bodies for light to live in —

see how colors catch the rays and hold them,
free them from the homelessness
of light's infinite journey as it arcs
and speeds otherwise eternally to nowhere.

Color lets light rest and simply be.

(3) Feel What the Life-Size Glass Swan Holds

I move my hand slowly
down the swan's neck,
which holds in a widening beam
the pale narrow light from the beak
as it loops long and earthward,
thickens as it slides and eases
down, a curve that darkens
toward the bulge and swell,
the muscle of potential flight.

Nothing I have ever touched
could hold these flight trajectories,
these smooth bends of shine
and wet, this swanness,
blown in glass two centuries ago
by the breath and hand of a

homesick Venetian craftsman
from a colony of glassmakers
bound by law to the island of Murano.

(4) *Ars Vitrica*

The makers who create out of glass, I learn,
make art without plan, not knowing the final shape,
color, spirit, or use of what they discover.
Their medium, appearing brittle and crystalline,
is really a super-cooled liquid, its molecules always
curving off like comets, always fluid and moving.
Which is why we can't cut glass, we can only
score and tap it to break it across its arcs.

Imagine such an artist coming to recognize slowly
the emerging idea in what's being made as she forms it,
reheating the lines as she works them,
keeping them liquid and flowing to somewhere,
somewhere. This is not mindless; it's the bending
of a sensual mind that's trained to explore,
sharply alert to growth and changes — so yes,
one more way to describe the art of making a poem.

An Encounter with Perhaps Miss Marianne Moore
in the Reading Room of the Library of Congress, 1966

Her hat cocked to the words
she is writing and reading,
the lady meets my scrutiny with the smile
of gracious queen to subject.
Bowing slightly, I return to my book,
preferring not to ask

if she is Miss Marianne Moore,
wanting to keep this clarity of eye and mind,
deciding not to mistrust
the triangular hat or the realness
of the red rose she has spirited here.
The rose signals class from a sparkling jelly jar.

I could test these impressions against
a book in the stacks on Marianne Moore
with frontispiece portrait. Instead I imagine
sending a schoolboy love-note across the aisle,
across thirty years, asking her out to lunch.
I want for some reason to carry the jar

without spilling a drop, the two of us
light on metro-gnomic feet,
up alphabetical A Street Southeast
to merely numerical Fifth
while she gives to each anonymous street
a possible, thoroughly proper name.

At the car I tell her, "I'll guide the wheel
of the '59 Falcon," and we cruise Independence
through traffic, failing to spot a Magicravure
on our way to Mike Palm's sports bar,
with Miss Moore nodding and noting,
"Without minuteness there can be no sublime."

1966; revised 2009

Looking at a Glass Jar Left in a House
Near the Baltimore Harbor

Left by the previous tenant, whom we never met,
stationed alone on the kitchen window sill,
a clean glass jar filled with sea shells. Moving out,
he must have wanted someone sitting here
having a drink, someone like us, to find at least
the shapes of some mysteries he had thought about
at this window, looking toward the harbor's lights —

the hardened shapes of oyster secretions,
mussel suction, claw of a shadowy sideways crab
along wet sands at sunset, secretive clams
shut tight and pulled about in the tide's
lunar pulse, shapes of all the other
wads of soft pink flesh that had run out of time.

But maybe he wanted someone to drift off —
as last night I did — from this glass column
to Fort McHenry's lights across the harbor
to think shells we call casings, shells expelled
from the breech that links technology
to death, casings strewn about the world's
killings, emptied in uniformed exchanges
across deserts or in urban cross-fire
through rubble streets — thuds, ripped flesh, Iraq,

mere shells of persons, of spent ex-lieutenants
discharged at last into gated cul de sacs
of fear, far beyond harbor and city streets.
And such a retreat, I now remember, is where
the landlord said this past tenant had moved to.

Washington Migrants

Still the birds follow the ancient maps
etched in their tiny brains as they arc
their long migrations. Instinct still
guides them to a stop in Washington.

I am watching a peaceful V-sign
of Canada geese, backlit by the Pentagon's
all-night lights, lower their landing gears,
slip on the oily Potomac, then break rank
and huddle among luxury power boats.

Up above, aluminum wings slice the sky,
taking turns for landings. I think of pterodactyls
circling the filled-in swamps under National Airport.
Now I hear a great wild honking —

it's the traffic on the bridges, edging out,
streaming towards the suburbs, signaling turns
in red with headlights dimmed, the daily homing
of thousands along routes that have paved over
the rest and peace the birds keep looking for.

1970; revised 2009

Remembering the Washington Race Riots, April 1968

It was a lonely way to watch
our city burn: high and still
in a friend's private plane, a Cherokee 360,
just circling, no race to anywhere,
carrying the name of a beaten people
to show off the power of our pistons.

We are chartered above the wild turbulence, above
the grief and black fists of our neighbors,
licensed by the colleges we're from,
held to a lawful pattern by an invisible beam
and a white hand tight on a stick.

The city below is foreign,
still as tomorrow's morning papers. We float,
stare as through ice at the bursting blooms of orange.

Look, we said to each other,
look how L'Enfant, bound by his geometric age,
tried to pattern everything — and left the rivers
and woods, the marshes and swamps down there
unmapped, like dark jagged wounds.
Those trim lines and circles of light at center,
those balanced angles shot with his transits,
were Reason's fear of disorder, and now
black rises up from inside it
and the forms are breaking and burning.
We were that close to understanding.

A voice crackles in from National Airport Control,
the state's concern that watches with care —
or with fear — our blips on a radar screen.
It asks and then again, *O-one-five-Romeo,*
what is your destination?
Under the red rotating light on top of the plane,
the pulse in the wrist of a guiding hand,
we are cruising far out and deaf for the moment

but soon to soar back
sleek in our pattern, hand on stick,
clenching an unspoken fear
that National Airport might be ablaze,
or otherwise sinking back to its natural past
in swamp fire, and in either case
no place for landing.

1968; revised 2010

Imagining Ezra Pound as My Uncle

I couldn't say why, from behind a reader's lectern that night,
I had called Pound "Uncle Ezra." But now I think of it, I like
to imagine having an Idaho uncle, fiery beard, exiled to Paris
and Venice, one who had strolled the horse-stink streets
of London in 1912 with Irish Yeats, Pound mumbling Greek
in pinned-up trousers of green pool-table felt while
railing against civilization's loss of decorum and order.

Admit you too would like an Uncle Ez the smug neighbors
will scorn, like him for when you're lonely and sometimes wonder.
Crank medievalist who hoarded his intersecting planes of light
in seven languages of glass and clay, a locomotive loose in a museum,
Pound moved through ill-lit rooms and dank, crumbling castles,
writing his rage against the bankers, Jews, and war.
He was ancient words, flying arms, shabby overcoat.
His answers to disorder, mostly paranoid, half-baked, and wrong,
are the twisted wreck of a derailed train on a dead-end spur line.

Still, we can sometimes hear in his startling lines, in new sounds,
a schizophrenia that only records our own, from deep down
in our culture. The indignant gods "who never left us" hesitate,
limp almost back to his call, but "will not return." I shake off his anger
and claim the uncle who as poet knows "they have never left us."
I claim as kin the carver who spent years tracking, like meteors
against the dark, the fragile curves of ideographic Chinese
nouns and verbs — the modernist who,
with a medieval alchemist's eye, found and hummed
a delicate "world of forms" in the very current and wire
and trembling filament of modern technology's electric street lamp.

"A blown husk," old Ezra called himself. For weeks he would lose
the power of speech — a relief to those who were nearest.
But he remembered "a pale flare over marshes," and the Madonna,
and Li Po's blowing sleeves. Beyond economics and the wrongs
for which we disown him, I take the long silences, a hush,
"a little light, like a rushlight, to lead back to splendor."

The Goat Trade

Etched now in the nation's memory will be the picture of the
stunned president . . . reading to school children from a book called
My Pet Goat.

The Washington Post

In our part of the planet we don't eat the meat
or look much into the yellow eyes of goats,
so we never really took to the nightmare stories

of evil power, goat's blood, or satanic dances.
The half-man-half-goat piper is all Greek to us,
could as well be from the other side of the moon.

Even the oversexed smelly old guy
who reminds us of the buck in rut
seems borrowed from a world of veils and tents.

Our own goats, now: they dance and sing, they
kneel on their knee-bones in meadows under stars,
they climb wire fences and carouse their way
through little colored books we read to our children.

As for goat marketing, we're good at that.
The ancients tanned the goatskins to make
wine sacks and parchment, and goat hairs
made fine little brushes for artists.

When they needed more than art to hold the mind
to what's beyond the flesh, monks would cut from goats
their hair shirts, rough and scratchy.

Since then we've raised the goat trade
to match the higher standards of our way of life.
Women shop for kid leather purses and gloves
and the softness of cashmere or angora stoles;

the yachtsman takes a touch of distinction
from sporting a goatee. And though eating goat

is still rare among us, we often permit our delicate palates
a small wedge of imported *chèvre* cheese.

Still. What is that lone black silhouette, with beard
and broken horn and bundle on its back,
that we see in flashes or dreams, feeling its way blind
as it escapes along the burning sands?**

**Surfacing sometimes from deep inside the Judeo-Christian *mythos* is the wandering goat. The ancient Hebrew high priest, on the annual Day of Atonement (Yom Kippur), would place upon the "scapegoat" all the sins of the nation and release it into the wilderness, bearing "all their iniquities unto a land not inhabited" (Leviticus 16).

Passing Through

Again today nothing
will happen again.
The woods creatures won't scare
at red on the moon
and at how the winds are reversed
and howling from inland.
Nothing hides from whatever
breathes hard up the dune.
Still, standing straight,
I wait for the possible terror
of the nothing at all
that by its nature
should not be able to be.

Monument: A Walled Garden in Barcelona

These were thin stripling vines when Picasso and Miro
walked this street. Columbus may have strode past
their seedlings. They grew thick on the south wall
in an installation Gaudi could have shaped: strained arms
of sailors clinging to broken planks; sealed dead buds
the scattered burial mounds for soldiers; a silver armada
running wayward, each ship a bead of water
that tacks its way down the limp pale stalks to strand itself
on gnarled wrists whose hands are digging deep
below the base of this statuary, into its foundation.

A small trumpet vine, blowing its springtime wine-red
hallelujah blasts, is off to the side in the resolving shade,
almost separate from the garden's monument to history.

West Window

What's out there past glass will go on without me —
gauzy green shoots or autumn blood in the trees,
deer on tip-toe in kneeling grasses and snow where boys
and girls had lain, strips of cloth dark against pale sand.
Close in, tadpoles and peepers will go on teeming under the arc
of a golden eagle slicing into the swamp across the road.

Up and down the shore that's beyond the dune, summer
neighbors will share drinks at four, lament wars and taxes,
dream through wild winds about waves ripping in too close,
shiver sometimes to see outlandish sunsets and shinings
and sails out past the whitecaps. They think for crazy moments
of the youngsters they were, or wanted to be, or had.

I try to gather the flash and hum and dark of everything
for a kind of hymn, a soft one, one that might rise daily
over the hairy ice-age dune out front, floating over
beachwear colors and staked boats on the beach to challenge
at the shore the shipwrecking lovely lake to some antiphonal singing
that I may almost have heard. Listen. It's closest in the still after
    storms.

Some Things I Try to Forget

That hot parrrot of Consuela's, one floor up,
squawks and shrieks down the atrium
just as I start to hear the sea slapping awake
San Juan's ancient sea wall. My voice makes a fist.

This reminds me of the time my grandpa, at his basement
workbench, talking to me softly like the Jesus he followed,
not like the progressive factory owner he was,
happened to hit his thumb with a hammer.

But far worse is to remember how once I woke
from a dream in which I had floated over a drowning town,
still lively with lights and little cars and waving trees
as it was sinking, and how I wanted to stay and watch.

Opening Up the Summer Lake Cottage in Early Spring

A dimple of mold
pock of emerald fur
little prayer of moss
kneeling at a lamp's base
as I switch on the season

too early. Household things
have become cold strangers
and testify against me.
I find a drawing, never framed,
yellowing in a stack of

old receipts: a tree
in India ink that checks
its ballet at the very edge
of flight, its curves poised
but uncertain, a get-well tree

brushed alive for me long ago
by my youngest son, then eleven,
the gifted fledgling who,
still uncertain, digs down
and seldom flies free.

In the dark of my shoes
my feet pilgrim from room
to room: memories, summer
shapes unready to speak,
the cold nurseries of mice.

After I can't make it back here,
Lord, let him imagine me
striding up the gravel drive
once each spring forever,
hoping he'll still hear me

saying his name as I
return to our old happy Eden

heading north to him
and his two brothers
coming back to open up.

Bethany Beach

Tonight, all along the Delaware shore, the ocean's lappings
wash and hush. The deathlike crash and moan
of the deep that hummed my mourning for forty summers
has now distanced itself like a son's black sail that has faded
into Greek mythology. He's gone. Wash and hush. Peace.

Five miles up the coast, this usual swirl of lights from Rehoboth
that flicker and blink. But now I remember what flings them upward —
the happy neon clink of penny arcades, ice cream stands,
little shops dealing T-shirts, surfboards, and sea-shell lamps.
Too distant for hearing now, the whirl of a joyful noise.

Still. This biblical beach where I sit remembers something.
Finally I'm hearing how waves out there could only repeat,
sighing their tired old line about grief: *He's lost, he's lost*
is all they've stuttered. But now, something like a call to *come forth*
from dark to the winking lights of a boardwalk holiday. I catch
from ages past (O taste and see) a salty sting in the nose
that rinses the mouth, it's the sea's old dance on the tongue
that smacks of icy raw oysters and a classic Athiri wine.

Winter Lightning

Washington streets these winter nights are cats,
dozing, one eye half open, watching for storms
while we citizens, deep in the certainty that lightning
never strikes until spring, are asleep.
But it strikes. It ripped into my dream one night
not as a jagged white spear but as sound,
a *shriek* as through homespun worsted,
shearing through a candle-lit room at the rear
of some foreign tailor shop, hunchbacked,
that I was peering into in my sleep.
That was a good year for making poems.

This stranger that wakes me as winter lightning
has other guises. It first came as the tall
and terrible angel who said to the child I was,
fear not. Twice in the decades after that, it threatened
chaos and death to what I tried to hold onto.
But now, an old man startled by late-in-life love,
I close my eyes to find it lighting up the soft dark
of this new millennium's dance of galaxies,
each one new, each a spark in a cat's eye nebula,
each spark tight with millions of spinning worlds.
This is a good year to rest, to watch, to be still.

Notes to Some of the Poems

p. 125: *The Pineapple Poem*

The reports of Gonzalo Fernandez de Oviedo to King Ferdinand are in the Huntington Library, San Marino, California. A translation of his long and exalting account of the pineapple can be found in J. L. Collins, *The Pineapple* (1960).

I have been delightfully convinced by my University of Maryland colleague Michael Olmert ("The Hospitable Pineapple," in *Colonial Williamsburg*, Winter 1997-98, 47-57) that the pineapple, in English and early American domestic arts, stood for much more than hospitality. Andrew Marvell's perception of the Cross was transmuted into a symbol for Christian charity and concern, the "idea of the common-weal and an all-encompassing regard for humanity." Not long after Marvell's poem "The Bermudas" was published in 1681, Sir Christopher Wren was devoutly working a pineapple motif in his churches.

Pineapple upside-down cake was a special dessert in the 1930s and 1940s.

I took on the challenge from Wallace Stevens, set forth in his esoteric lecture "Someone Puts a Pineapple Together," warning that the pineapple makes "its invitation to false metaphor." Not always, I'd say. But by far the greatest challenge in writing this encomium is that the pineapple is the only food in the world I detest. This celebration of it was intended to convince my students (see especially the second stanza) that the right words and the working imagination can create a reality that transcends the limitations of merely actual personal taste. The suggested writing assignment: *celebrate something you hate;* this forces the poet to *create* what is not yet known to her rather than merely *reporting without discovery* what she likes and already knows.

p. 136: *We Used to Grade God's Sunsets from the Lost Valley Beach*

Some three years after writing this poem, a trifle worried about its possible irreverence, I happened into the Jerusalem Bible's translation of the eighth chapter of Saint Paul's Letter to the Romans. In this translation at least, Saint Paul's theology corroborates my instincts. I decided to use a piece of it as an epigraph for Part I.

Our fear of His weather howling through the galaxies: "The solar wind . . . expands continuously outward at velocities of about 1 million mph or more. It hollows out a sort of bubble in which the sun and its planets plow through the interstellar medium" (Kathy Sawyer in *The Washington Post*).

p. 149: *Bix Beiderbecke Composing Light, 1927-1931*

Jazzman Bix Beiderbecke (1903-1931), legendary hot cornetist who never learned to read music well at all, worked feverishly in the final days before his death at 28 on the last two of his compositions for piano. Remarkably (though never remarked upon by him), all the titles have to do with the perception of light.

pp. 160-67: *Up from the Borinage: Three for Vincent Van Gogh*

North Brabant is the province in the Netherlands in which Van Gogh was born and raised, where his grandfather and his father were pastors in the Netherlands Reformed Church. In young manhood he lived there off and on, uneasily. His early sketches and paintings of Brabant farm laborers and poor weavers culminated in his first masterpiece, *The Potato Eaters*.

Drenthe is a province in the north of the Netherlands.

The Borinage is a district in southern Belgium near the French border where the young Van Gogh served as an unpaid missionary-pastor, living among poor and miserably exploited coal miners and their families. Before he was removed by his superiors, he had begun making sketches, mostly of the workers.

In "Van Gogh, Talking to Himself . . ." all phrases in italics are quoted from Van Gogh's letters. The rest of the poem, using paraphrase and echoing, is created exactly from these same letters.

Auvers-sur-Oise is the town near Paris where Van Gogh spent his last three months, after the creative surge and the breakdowns and the "attacks" he experienced at Arles, in Provence. Correcting popular belief, the letters from here reflect not despair, but a growing peace and calm, and the last paintings are remarkable for their renewed reliance upon black — suggesting, as do the letters, not so much madness and morbidity as a restoring fullness and depth. Van Gogh died at Auvers of a self-inflicted gunshot wound on July 28, 1890, at age 37.

Theo Van Gogh, Vincent's younger brother, recipient of 3,000 letters, was an art dealer (as were three of Van Gogh's uncles). Theo sent Vincent money regularly, but sold only two of the hundreds of Vincent's pictures in his possession. The letters do not bear out our current romanticized legend of two loving brothers. Vincent was grateful but ambivalent. When Theo wrote Vincent the then-popular notion that painters should not use the color black, Vincent explained with great restraint and patience that darkness has lights in it and that there are, for example, twenty-seven shades of black in the paintings of Franz Hals.

"Strangers in the Earth" is the first — and the only surviving — sermon by Van Gogh. He preached it in London in 1876, at age 23.

pp. 160-67: *Assignment Nicaragua, 1985*

The six poems here are worked from a diary I kept, in December 1984 and January 1985, while gathering data in Nicaragua as a volunteer with a Witness for Peace delegation. I wrote a two-part report on the war between the Sandinistas and the U.S.-supported Contras for the *Reformed Journal* (summer of 1985). Some of the unforgettable images roughly sketched in the diary found their way into these poems many years later.

pp. 169-71: *In the Red Sea: Snorkeling off Basata*

Basata is located on the arm of the Red Sea called the Gulf of Aqaba. The Sinai Desert, scattered with rusting military wrecks, is immediately behind it, and Saudi Arabia is clearly visible across the water to the east. The poem is set a few days before the outbreak of the Persian Gulf War, the American army's buildup for which is at its peak.

p. 173: *Ending the Nationwide Poets' Strike*

My friend Paul Zimmer carried a conversation of ours into a mock-serious poem calling all American poets to go on strike. See his book *The Great Bird of Love* (University of Illinois Press, 1989), p. 33.

This is a sequel. The numbers for exclamation points and plastic lawn ornaments are from an issue of *Harper's Index*.

p. 174: *Proposing the Text for a United States National War Memorial*

The coincidence of the beginning of a new war in Iraq and the opening of Washington's huge and pompous memorial to an old one, World War II, brought to mind the great lines I quote from James Agee. In contrast to Agee's lines, and also to the adjacent Viet Nam War Memorial, the World War II Memorial feels like the kind of architecture and sculpture that Albert Speer might have recommended to Adolph Hitler. Big, ponderous, heavy salutes to might — and words carved in stone that are not otherwise memorable.

The words *screens* and *monitors* occur because the poem was originally written for distribution online on the Web site www.poetsagainst thewar.org.

p. 196: *Credence*

Video quia credo — "I see because I believe" — deliberately reverses the popular saying "Seeing is believing." *Credo quia absurdum est* — "I believe because it is absurd" — is a controversial formulation made famous by St. Anselm. I sometimes agree.

p. 216: *Fishing Up Words in Norway*

I have never been to Norway. I hope this strengthens the point of the poem.

p. 225: *An Encounter with Perhaps Miss Marianne Moore in the Reading Room of the Library of Congress, 1966*

Marianne Moore (1887-1972), who confirmed later by letter that it was indeed she that I had seen that day, had been hired by the Ford Motor Company to suggest possible names for a new car of theirs. *Magicravure* is one of a dozen or so imaginative names that she proposed for what was to be named the ill-fated *Edsel*.

Acknowledgments

The poems in the first three sections of this book originally appeared in three books published by Dryad Press (Washington and San Francisco). I am grateful to Dryad Press for permission to reprint them here. The books are *Something Tugging the Line* (1974), *The Lost Faces* (1979), and *The Eighth Day: New and Selected Poems* (1984).

The translations from the Frisian language in the fourth section were originally published in two bilingual books by William B. Eerdmans Publishing Company: *Country Fair: Poems from Friesland since 1945* (1985), and *The Sound that Remains: A Historical Collection of Frisian Poetry* (1990). The translations from modern Hebrew in this section are by Moshe Dor and Rod Jellema and are published here for the first time.

The poems in section five are from my collection titled *A Slender Grace,* published in 2004 by Eerdmans.

Many of the new poems in the sixth section, titled "Still . . . Later Poems, 2005-2010," were published — sometimes in earlier versions — in the following journals: *Image, Poetry Northwest, Delmarva Review, Many Mountains Moving, International Poetry Review, Vineyard, Innisfree Poetry Journal, ARTS, Faculty Voice* (University of Maryland), *Hawaii Pacific Review, Baltimore Review, Mare Nostrum, Poet Lore, Spiritus,* and *Potomac Review.* I am grateful to the editors of these publications.

My thanks to five poet friends who gave their astute critical readings to some of these poems and their general encouragement to the whole book: Marie Pavlicek-Wehrli, Martin Galvin, Moshe Dor, Christina Daub, and Kevin Craft. Thanks also to Professor Mark Burrows for the friendly sharing of insights that kept the last section of this book alive. And finally my thanks to the writers in my last three workshops at the Writers Center, Bethesda, Maryland, who reminded me how it's done.

My wife, Michele Orwin, has been the toughest and most valuable critic of the new poems in this book. Without her high expectations and constant encouragement, those poems and thus the book as a whole would not exist.

CD Track List